IN THE MONSTER'S CLUTCHES.
Body and Brain on Fire.

GRAPPLING WITH THE MONSTER

OR

THE CURSE AND THE CURE OF STRONG DRINK

BY

T. S. ARTHUR

AUTHOR OF "TEN NIGHTS IN A BAR-ROOM," "THREE YEARS IN A MAN-TRAP," "CAST ADRIFT," "DANGER," ETC.

NEW YORK
JOHN W. LOVELL COMPANY
142 TO 150 WORTH STREET

INTRODUCTION.

IN preparing this, his latest volume, the author found himself embarrassed from the beginning, because of the large amount of material which came into his hands, and the consequent difficulty of selection and condensation. There is not a chapter which might not have been extended to twice its present length, nor a fact stated, or argument used, which might not have been supplemented by many equally pertinent and conclusive. The extent to which alcohol curses the whole people cannot be shown in a few pages: the sad and terrible history would fill hundreds of volumes. And the same may be said of the curse which this poisonous substance lays upon the souls and bodies of men. Fearful as is the record which will be found in the chapters devoted to the curse of drink, let the reader bear in mind that a thousandth part has not been told.

In treating of the means of reformation, prevention and cure, our effort has been to give to each agency the largest possible credit for what it is doing. There is no movement, organization or work, however broad or limited in its sphere, which has for its object the cure of drunkenness in the individual, or the suppression of the liquor traffic in the State, that is not contributing its measure of service to the great cause every true temperance advocate has at heart; and what we largely need is, toleration for those who do not see with us, nor act with us in our special methods. Let us never forget the Divine admonition—"Forbid him not: for he that is not against us is for us."

Patience, toleration and self-repression are of vital importance in any good cause. If we cannot see with another, let us be careful that, by opposition, we do not cripple him in his work. If we can assist him by friendly counsel to clearer seeing, or, by a careful study of his methods, gain a large efficiency for our own, far more good will be done than by hard antagonism, which rarely helps, and too surely blinds and hinders.

Our book treats of the curse and cure of drunkenness. How much better not to come under the terrible curse! How much better to run no risks where the malady is so disastrous, and the cure so difficult!

To young men who are drifting easily into the dangerous drinking habits of society, we earnestly commend the chapters in which will be found the medical testimony against alcohol, and also the one on "The Growth and Power of Appetite." They will see that it is impossible for a man to use alcoholic drinks regularly without laying the foundation for both physical and mental diseases, and, at the same time, lessening his power to make the best of himself in his life-work; while beyond this lies the awful risk of acquiring an appetite which may enslave, degrade and ruin him, body and soul, as it is dedegrading and ruining its tens of thousands yearly.

It is sincerely hoped that many may be led by the facts here presented, to grapple with the monster and to thus promote his final overthrow.

CONTENTS.

CHAPTER IX.

CHAPTER X.

CHAPTER XI.

CHAPTER XII.

CHAPTER XIII.

CHAPTER XIV.

CHAPTER XV.

CHAPTER XVI.

CHAPTER XVII.

CHAPTER XVIII.

LIST OF ILLUSTRATIONS.

"*Woe unto him that giveth his neighbor drink, that puttest thy bottle to him, and makest him drunken also.*"—HABAKKUK ii, 15.

CHAPTER I.

THE MONSTER, STRONG DRINK.

THERE are two remarkable passages in a very old book, known as the Proverbs of Solomon, which cannot be read too often, nor pondered too deeply. Let us quote them here:

1. "Wine is a mocker, strong drink is raging; and whosoever is deceived thereby is not wise.

2. "Who hath woe? who hath sorrow? who hath contentions? who hath babblings? who hath wounds without cause? who hath redness of eyes? They that tarry long at the wine; they that go to seek mixed wine. Look not thou upon the wine when it is red, when it giveth his color in the cup, when it moveth itself aright. At the last it biteth like a serpent and stingeth like an adder."

It is many thousands of years since this record was made, and to-day, as in that far distant age of the world, wine is a mocker, and strong drink raging; and still, as then, they who tarry long at the wine; who go to seek mixed wine, discover that, "*at the last*," it biteth like a serpent and stingeth like an adder.

This mocking and raging! These bitings and stingings! These woes and woundings! Alas, for the exceeding bitter cry of their pain, which is heard above every other cry of sorrow and suffering.

ALCOHOL AN ENEMY.

The curse of strong drink! Where shall we begin, where end, or how, in the clear and truthful sentences that wrest conviction from doubt, make plain the allegations we shall bring against an enemy that is sowing disease, poverty, crime and sorrow throughout the land?

Among our most intelligent, respectable and influential people, this enemy finds a welcome and a place of honor. Indeed, with many he is regarded as a friend and treated as such. Every possible opportunity is given him to gain favor in the household and with intimate and valued friends. He is given the amplest confidence and the largest freedom; and he always repays this confidence with treachery and spoliation; too often blinding and deceiving his victims while his work of robbery goes on. He is not only a robber, but a cruel master; and his bondsmen and abject slaves are to be found in hundreds and thousands, and even tens of thousands, of our homes, from the poor dwelling of the day-laborer, up to the palace of the merchant-prince.

PLACE AND POWER IN THE HOUSEHOLD.

Of this fact no one is ignorant; and yet, strange to tell, large numbers of our most intelligent, respectable and influential people continue to smile upon this enemy; to give him place and power in their households, and to cherish him as a friend; but with this singular reserve of thought and purpose, that he is to be trusted just so far and no farther. He is so pleasant and genial, that, for the sake of his favor, they are ready to encounter the risk of his acquiring, through the license they afford, the vantage-ground of a pitiless enemy!

But, it is not only in their social life that the people hold this enemy in favorable regard, and give him the opportunity to hurt and destroy. Our great Republic has entered into a compact with him, and, for a money-consideration, given him the

FREEDOM OF THE NATION;

so that he can go up and down the land at will And not only has our great Republic done this but the States of which it is composed, with only one or two exceptions, accord to him the same freedom. Still more surprising, in almost every town and city, his right to plunder, degrade, enslave and destroy the people has been established under the safe guarantee of law.

Let us give ourselves to the sober consideration of what we are suffering at his hands, and take measures of defense and safety, instead of burying our heads in the sand, like the foolish ostrich, while the huntsmen are sweeping down upon us.

ENORMOUS CONSUMPTION.

Only those who have given the subject careful consideration have any true idea of the enormous annual consumption, in this country, of spirits, wines and malt liquors. Dr. Hargreaves, in "Our Wasted Resources," gives these startling figures: It amounted in 1870 to 72,425,353 gallons of domestic spirits, 188,527,120 gallons of fermented liquors, 1,441,747 gallons of imported spirits, 9,088,894 gallons of wines, 34,239 gallons of spirituous compounds, and 1,012,754 gallons of ale, beer, etc., or a total of 272,530,107 gallons for 1870, with a total increase of 30,000,000 gallons in 1871, and of 35,000,000 gallons in addition in 1872.

All this in a single year, and at a cost variously estimated at from six to seven hundred millions of dollars! Or, a sum, as statistics tell us, nearly equal to the cost of all the flour, cotton and woolen goods, boots and shoes, clothing, and books and newspapers purchased by the people in the same period of time.

If this were all the cost? If the people wasted no more than seven hundred millions of dollars on these beverages every year, the question of their use would be only one of pecuniary loss or gain. But what farther, in connection with this subject, are we told by statistics? Why, that, in consequence of using these beverages, we have six hundred thousand drunkards; and that of these, sixty thousand die every year. That we have over three hundred murders and four hundred suicides. That over two hundred thousand children are left homeless and friendless. And that at least eighty per cent. of all the crime and pauperism of the land arises from the consumption of this enormous quantity of intoxicating drinks.

In this single view, the question of intemperance assumes a most appalling aspect. The

POVERTY AND DESTITUTION

found in so large a portion of our laboring classes, and their consequent restlessness and discontent, come almost entirely from the waste of substance, idleness and physical incapacity for work, which attend the free use of alcoholic beverages. Of the six or seven hundred millions of dollars paid annually for these beverages, not less than two-thirds are taken out of the earnings of our artisans and laborers, and those who, like them, work for wages.

LOSS TO LABOR.

But the loss does not, of course, stop here. The consequent waste of bodily vigor, and the idleness that is ever the sure accompaniment of drinking, rob this class of at least as much more. Total abstinence societies, building associations, and the use of banks for savings, instead of the dram-sellers' banks for losings, would do more for the well-being of our working classes than all the trades-unions or labor combinations, that ever have or ever will exist. The laboring man's protective union lies in his own good common sense, united with temperance, self-denial and economy. There are very many in our land who know this way; and their condition, as compared with those who know it not, or knowing, will not walk therein, is found to be in striking contrast.

TAXATION.

Besides the wasting drain for drink, and the loss in national wealth, growing out of the idleness and diminished power for work, that invariably follows the use of alcohol in any of its forms, the people are heavily taxed for the repression and punishment of crimes, and the support of paupers and destitute children. A fact or two will give the reader some idea of what this enormous cost must be. In "The Twentieth Annual Report of the Executive Committee of the Prison Association of New York," is this sentence: "There can be no doubt that, of all the proximate sources of crime, the use of intoxicating liquors is the most prolific and the most deadly. Of other causes it may be said that they slay their thousands; of this it may be acknowledged that it slays its tens of thousands. The committee asked for the opinion of the jail officers in nearly every county in the State as to the proportion of commitments due, either directly or indirectly, to strong drink."

The whole number of commitments is given in these words: "Not less than 60,000 to 70,000 [or the sixtieth portion of the inhabitants of the State of New York] human beings—men, women and children—either guilty, or arrested on suspicion of being guilty of crime, pass every year through these institutions." The answers made to the committee by the jail officers, varied from two-thirds as the lowest, to nine-tenths as the highest; and, on taking the average of their figures, it gave seven-eighths as the proportion of commitments for crime directly ascribed to the use of intoxicating drinks!

Taking this as the proportion of those who are made criminals through intemperance, let us get at some estimate of the cost to tax-payers. We find it stated in Tract No. 28, issued by the National Temperance Society, that "a committee was appointed by the Ulster County Temperance Society, in 1861, for the express purpose of ascertaining, from reliable sources, the percentage on every dollar tax paid to the county to support her paupers and criminal justice. The committee, after due examination, came to the conclusion that upwards of sixty cents on the dollar was for the above purpose. This amount was required, *according to law*, to be paid by every tax-payer as a *penalty, or rather as a rum bill*, for allowing the liquor traffic to be carried on in the above county. What is said of Ulster County, may, more or less, if a like examination were entered into, be said of every other county, not only in the State of New York, but in every county in the United States."

From the same tract we take this statement: "In a document published by the Legislature of the State of New York, for 1863, being the report of the Secretary of the State to the Legislature, we have the following statements: 'The whole number of paupers relieved during the same period, was 261,252. During the year 1862, 257,354.' These numbers would be in the ratio of one pauper annually to every fifteen inhabitants throughout the State. In an examination made into the history of those paupers by a competent committee, *seven-eighths of them were reduced* to this low and degraded condition, directly or indirectly, through intemperance."

CURSING THE POOR.

Looking at our laboring classes, with the fact before us, that the cost of the liquor sold annually by retail dealers is equal to nearly $25 for every man, woman and child in our whole population, and we can readily see why so much destitution is to be found among them. Throwing out those who abstain altogether; the children, and a large proportion of women, and those who take a glass only now and then, and it will be seen that for the rest the average of cost must be more than treble. Among working men who drink the cheaper beverages, the ratio of cost to each cannot fall short of a hundred dollars a year. With many, drink consumes from a fourth to one-half of their entire earnings. Is it, then, any wonder that so much poverty and suffering are to be found among them?

CRIME AND PAUPERISM.

The causes that produce crime and pauperism in our own country, work the same disastrous results in other lands where intoxicants are used. An

WOE
UNTO
YOU
ALSO . . .
FOR YE
LADE
MEN
WITH
BURDENS
GRIEVOUS
TO BE
BORNE.
LUKE xi, 46.

HEAPING BURDENS UPON POVERTY.

WOE
UNTO
HIM
THAT
GIVETH HIS
NEIGHBOR
DRINK,
THAT
PUTTEST
THY
BOTTLE
TO HIM.
HAB. ii, 15.

English writer, speaking of the sad effects of intemperance in Great Britain, says: "One hundred million pounds, which is now annually wasted, is a sum as great as was spent in seven years upon all the railways of the kingdom—in the very heyday of railway projects; a sum so vast, that if saved annually, for seven years, would blot out the national debt!" Another writer says, "that in the year 1865, over £6,000,000, or a tenth part of the whole national revenue, was required to support her paupers." Dr. Lees, of London, in speaking of Ireland, says: "Ireland has been a poor nation from want of capital, and has wanted capital chiefly because the people have preferred swallowing it to saving it." The Rev. G. Holt, chaplain of the Birmingham Workhouse, says: "From my own experience, I am convinced of the accuracy of a statement made by the late governor, that of every one hundred persons admitted, ninety-nine were reduced to this state of humiliation and dependence, either directly or indirectly, through the prevalent and ruinous drinking usages."

Mr. Charles Buxton, M. P., in his pamphlet, "How to Stop Drunkenness," says: "It would not be too much to say that if all drinking of fermented liquors could be done away, crime of every kind would fall to a fourth of its present amount, and the whole tone of moral feeling in the lower order might be indefinitely raised. Not only does this vice produce all kinds of wanton mischief, but it has also a negative effect of great importance. It is the mightiest of all the forces that clog the progress of good. * * * The struggle of the school, the library and the church, all united against the beer-shop and the gin-palace, is but one development of the war between Heaven and hell. It is, in short, intoxication that fills our jails; it is intoxication that fills our lunatic asylums; it is intoxication that fills our work-houses with poor. Were it not for this one cause, pauperism would be nearly extinguished in England."

THE BLIGHT EVERYWHERE.

We could go on and fill pages with corroborative facts and figures, drawn from the most reliable sources. But these are amply sufficient to show the extent and magnitude of the curse which the liquor traffic has laid upon our people. Its blight is everywhere—on our industries, on our social life; on our politics, and even on our religion.

And, now, let us take the individual man himself, and see in what manner this treacherous enemy deals with him when he gets him into his power.

CHAPTER II.

IT CURSES THE BODY.

FIRST as to the body. One would suppose, from the marred and scarred, and sometimes awfully disfigured forms and faces of men who have indulged in intoxicating drinks, which are to be seen everywhere and among all classes of society, that there would be no need of other testimony to show that alcohol is an enemy to the body. And yet, strange to say, men of good sense, clear judgment and quick perception in all moral questions and in the general affairs of life, are often so blind, or infatuated here, as to affirm that this substance, alcohol, which they use under the various forms of wine, brandy, whisky, gin, ale or beer, is not only harmless, when taken in moderation—each being his own judge as to what "moderation" means—but actually useful and nutritious!

Until within the last fifteen or twenty years, a large proportion of the medical profession not only favored this view, but made constant prescription of alcohol in one form or another, the sad results of which too often made their appearance in exascerbations of disease, or in the formation of intemperate habits among their patients. Since then, the chemist and the physiologist have subjected alcohol to the most rigid tests, carried on often for years, and with a faithfulness that could not be satisfied with guess work, or inference, or hasty conclusion.

ALCOHOL NOT A FOOD AND OF DOUBTFUL USE AS A MEDICINE.

As a result of these carefully-conducted and long-continued examinations and experiments, the medical profession stands to-day almost as a unit against alcohol; and makes solemn public declaration to the people that it "is not shown to have a definite food value by any of the usual methods of chemical analysis or physiological investigations;" and that as a medicine its range is very limited, admitting often of a substitute, and that it should never be taken unless prescribed by a physician.

Reports of these investigations to which we have referred have appeared, from time to time, in the medical journals of Europe and America, and their results are now embodied in many of the standard and most reliable treatises and text-books of the medical profession.

In this chapter we shall endeavor to give our readers a description of the changes and deteriorations which take place in the blood, nerves, membranes, tissues and organs, in consequence of the continued introduction of alcohol into the human body; and in doing so, we shall quote freely from medical writers, in order that our readers may have the testimony before them in its directest form, and so be able to judge for themselves as to its value.

DIGESTION.

And here, in order to give those who are not familiar with the process of digestion, a clear idea of that important operation, and the effect produced when alcohol is taken with food, we quote from the lecture of an English physician, Dr. Henry Monroe, on "The Physiological Action of Alcohol." He says:

"Every kind of substance employed by man as food consists of sugar, starch, oil and glutinous matters, mingled together in various proportions; these are designed for the support of the animal frame. The glutinous principles of food—*fibrine*, *albumen* and *casein*—are employed to build up the structure; while the *oil*, *starch* and *sugar* are chiefly used to generate heat in the body.

"The first step of the digestive process is the breaking up of the food in the mouth by means of the jaws and teeth. On this being done, the saliva, a viscid liquor, is poured into the mouth from the salivary glands, and as it mixes with the food, it performs a very important part in the operation of digestion, rendering the starch of the food soluble, and gradually changing it into a sort of sugar, after which the other principles become more miscible with it. Nearly a pint of saliva is furnished every twenty-four hours for the use of an adult. When the food has been masticated and mixed with the saliva, it is then passed into the stomach, where it is acted upon by a juice secreted by the filaments of that organ, and poured into the stomach in large quantities whenever food comes in contact with its mucous coats. It consists of a dilute acid known to the chemists as hydrochloric acid, composed of hydrogen and chlorine, united together in certain definite proportions. The gastric juice contains, also, a peculiar organic-ferment or decomposing substance, containing nitrogen—something of the nature of yeast—termed *pepsine*, which is easily soluble in the acid just named. That gastric juice acts as a simple chemical solvent, is proved by the fact that, after death, it has been known to dissolve the stomach itself.

ALCOHOL RETARDS DIGESTION.

"It is an error to suppose that, after a good dinner, a glass of spirits or beer assists digestion; or that any liquor containing alcohol—even bitter beer—can in any way assist digestion. Mix some bread and meat with gastric juice; place them in a phial, and keep that phial in a sand-bath at the slow heat of 98 degrees, occasionally shaking briskly the contents to imitate the motion of the stomach; you will find, after six or eight hours, the whole contents blended into one pultaceous mass. If to another phial of food and gastric juice, treated in the same way, I add a glass of pale ale or a quantity of alcohol, at the end of seven or eight hours, or even some days, the food is scarcely acted upon at all. This is a fact; and if you are led to ask why, I answer, because alcohol has the peculiar power of chemically affecting or decomposing the gastric juice by precipitating one of its principal constituents, viz., pepsine, rendering its solvent properties much less efficacious. Hence alcohol can not be considered either as food or as a solvent for food. Not as the latter certainly, for it refuses to act with the gastric juice.

"'It is a remarkable fact,' says Dr. Dundas Thompson, 'that alcohol, when added to the digestive fluid, produces a white precipitate, so that the fluid is no longer capable of digesting animal or vegetable matter.' 'The use of alcoholic stimulants,' say Drs. Todd and Bowman, 'retards digestion by coagulating the pepsine, an essential element of the gastric juice, and thereby interfering with its action. Were it not that wine and spirits are rapidly absorbed, the introduction of these into the stomach, in any quantity, would be a complete bar to the digestion of food, as the pepsine would be precipitated from the solution as quickly as it was formed by the stomach.' Spirit, in any quantity, as a dietary adjunct, is pernicious on account of its antiseptic qualities, which resist the digestion of food by the absorption of water from its particles, in direct antagonism to chemical operation."

ITS EFFECT ON THE BLOOD.

Dr. Richardson, in his lectures on alcohol, given both in England and America, speaking of the action of this substance on the blood after passing from the stomach, says:

"Suppose, then, a certain measure of alcohol be taken into the stomach, it will be absorbed there, but, previous to absorption, it will have to undergo a proper degree of dilution with water, for there is this peculiarity respecting alcohol when it is separated by an animal membrane from a watery fluid like the blood, that it will not pass through the membrane until it has become charged, to a given point of dilution, with water. It is itself, in fact, *so greedy for water, it will pick it up from watery textures, and deprive them of it until, by its saturation, its power of reception is exhausted,* after which it will diffuse into the current of circulating fluid."

It is this power of absorbing water from every texture with which alcoholic spirits comes in contact, that creates the burning thirst of those who freely indulge in its use. Its effect, when it reaches the circulation, is thus described by Dr. Richardson:

"As it passes through the circulation of the lungs it is exposed to the air, and some little of it, raised into vapor by the natural heat, is thrown off in expiration. If the quantity of it be large, this loss may be considerable, and the odor of the spirit may be detected in the expired breath. If the quantity be small, the loss will be comparatively little, as the spirit will be held in solution by the water in the blood. After it has passed through the lungs, and has been driven by the left heart over the arterial circuit, it passes into what is called the minute circulation, or the structural circulation of the organism. The arteries here extend into very small vessels, which are called arterioles, and from these infinitely small vessels spring the equally minute radicals or roots of the veins, which are ultimately to become the great rivers bearing the blood back to the heart. In its passage through this minute circulation the alcohol finds its way to every organ. To this brain, to these muscles, to these secreting or excreting organs, nay, even into this bony structure itself, it moves with the blood. In some of these parts which are not excreting, it remains for a time diffused, and in those parts where there is a large percentage of water, it remains longer than in other parts. From some organs which have an open tube for conveying fluids away, as the liver and kidneys, it is thrown out or eliminated, and in this way a portion of it is ultimately removed from the body. The rest passing round and round with the circulation, is probably decomposed and carried off in new forms of matter.

"When we know the course which the alcohol takes in its passage through the body, from the period of its absorption to that of its elimination, we are the better able to judge what physical changes it induces in the different organs and structures with which it comes in contact. It first reaches the blood; but, as a rule, the quantity of it that enters is insufficient to produce any material effect on that fluid. If, however, the dose taken be poisonous or semi-poisonous, then even the blood, rich as it is in water—and it contains seven hundred and ninety parts in a thousand—is affected. The alcohol is diffused through this water, and there it comes in contact with the other constituent parts, with the fibrine, that plastic substance which, when blood is drawn, clots and coagulates, and which is present in the proportion of from two to three parts in a thousand; with the albumen which exists in the proportion of seventy parts; with the salts which yield about ten parts; with the fatty matters; and lastly, with those minute, round bodies which float in myriads in the blood (which were discovered by the Dutch philosopher, Leuwenhock, as one of the first results of microscopical observation, about the middle of the seventeenth century), and which are called the blood globules or corpuscles. These last-named bodies are, in fact, cells; their discs, when natural, have a smooth outline, they are depressed in the centre, and they are red in color; the color of the blood being derived from them. We have discovered in recent years that there exist other corpuscles or cells in the blood in much smaller quantity, which are called white cells, and these different cells float in the blood-stream within the vessels. The red take the centre of the stream; the white lie externally near the sides of the vessels, moving less quickly. Our business is mainly with the red corpuscles. They perform the most important functions in the economy; they absorb, in great part, the oxygen which we inhale in breathing, and carry it to the extreme tissues of the body; they absorb, in great part, the carbonic acid gas which is produced in the combustion of the body in the extreme tissues, and bring that gas back to the lungs to be exchanged for oxygen there; in short, they are the vital instruments of the circulation.

"With all these parts of the blood, with the water, fibrine, albumen, salts, fatty matter and corpuscles, the alcohol comes in contact when it enters the blood, and, if it be in sufficient quantity, it produces disturbing action. I have watched this disturbance very carefully on the blood corpuscles; for, in some animals we can see these floating along during life, and we can also observe them from men who are under the effects of alcohol, by removing a speck of blood, and examining it with the microscope. The action of the alcohol, when it is observable, is varied. It may cause the corpuscles to run too closely together, and to adhere in rolls; it may modify their outline, making the clear-defined, smooth, outer edge irregular or crenate, or even starlike; it may change the round corpuscle into the oval form, or, in very extreme cases, it may produce what I may call a truncated form of corpuscles, in which the change is so great that if we did not trace it through all its stages, we should be puzzled to know whether the object looked at were indeed a blood-cell. All these changes are due to the action of the spirit upon the water contained in the corpuscles; upon the capacity of the spirit to extract water from them. During every stage of modification of corpuscles thus described, their function to absorb and fix gases is impaired, and when the aggregation of the cells, in masses, is great, other difficulties arise, for the cells, united together, pass less easily than they should through the minute vessels of the lungs and of the general circulation, and impede the current, by which local injury is produced.

"A further action upon the blood, instituted by alcohol in excess, is upon the fibrine or the plastic colloidal matter. On this the spirit may act in two different ways, according to the degree in which it affects the water that holds the fibrine in solution. It may fix the water with the fibrine, and thus destroy the power of coagulation; or it may extract the water so determinately as to produce coagulation."

ON THE MINUTE CIRCULATION.

The doctor then goes on to describe the minute circulation through which the constructive material in the blood is distributed to every part of the body. "From this distribution of blood in these minute vessels," he says, "the structure of organs derive their constituent parts; through these vessels brain matter, muscle, gland, membrane, are given out from the blood by a refined process of selection of material, which, up to this time, is only so far understood as to enable us to say that it exists. The minute and intermediate vessels are more intimately connected than any other part with the construction and with the function of the living matter of which the body is composed. Think you that this mechanism is left uncontrolled? No; the vessels, small as they are, are under distinct control. Infinitely refined in structure, they nevertheless have the power of contraction and dilatation, which power is governed by nervous action of a special kind."

Now, there are certain chemical agents, which, by their action on the nerves, have the power to paralyze and relax these minute blood-vessels, at their extreme points. "The whole series of nitrates," says Dr. Richardson, "possess this power; ether possesses it; but the great point I wish to bring forth is, that the substance we are specially dealing with, alcohol, possesses the self-same power. By this influence it produces all those peculiar effects which in every-day life are so frequently illustrated."

PARALYZES THE MINUTE BLOOD-VESSELS.

It paralyzes the minute blood-vessels, and allows them to become dilated with the flowing blood.

"If you attend a large dinner party, you will observe, after the first few courses, when the wine is beginning to circulate, a progressive change in some of those about you who have taken wine.

The face begins to get flushed, the eye brightens, and the murmur of conversation becomes loud. What is the reason of that flushing of the countenance? It is the same as the flush from blushing, or from the reaction of cold, or from the nitrite of amyl. It is the dilatation of vessels following upon the reduction of nervous control, which reduction has been induced by the alcohol. In a word, the first stage, the stage of vascular excitement from alcohol, has been established.

HEART DISTURBANCE.

"The action of the alcohol extending so far does not stop there. With the disturbance of power in the extreme vessels, more disturbance is set up in other organs, and the first organ that shares in it is the heart. With each beat of the heart a certain degree of resistance is offered by the vessels when their nervous supply is perfect, and the stroke of the heart is moderated in respect both to tension and to time. But when the vessels are rendered relaxed, the resistance is removed, the heart begins to run quicker, like a watch from which the pallets have been removed, and the heart-stroke, losing nothing in force, is greatly increased in frequency, with a weakened recoil stroke. It is easy to account, in this manner, for the quickened heart and pulse which accompany the first stage of deranged action from alcohol, and you will be interested to know to what extent this increase of vascular action proceeds.

The information on this subject is exceedingly curious and important."

* * * * * * * *

"The stage of primary excitement of the circulation thus induced lasts for a considerable time, but at length the heart flags from its overaction, and requires the stimulus of more spirit to carry it on in its work. Let us take what we may call a moderate amount of alcohol, say two ounces by volume, in form of wine, or beer, or spirits. What is called strong sherry or port may contain as much as twenty-five per cent. by volume. Brandy over fifty; gin, thirty-eight; rum, forty-eight; whisky, forty-three; vin ordeinaire, eight; strong ale, fourteen; champagne, ten to eleven; it matters not which, if the quantity of alcohol be regulated by the amount present in the liquor imbibed. When we reach the two ounces, a distinct physiological effect follows, leading on to that first stage of excitement with which we are now conversant. The reception of the spirit arrested at this point, there need be no important mischief done to the organism; but if the quantity imbibed be increased, further changes quickly occur. We have seen that all the organs of the body are built upon the vascular structures, and therefore it follows that a prolonged paralysis of the minute circulation must of necessity lead to disturbance in other organs than the heart.

OTHER ORGANS INVOLVED.

"By common observation, the flush seen on the cheek during the first stage of alcoholic excitation, is presumed to extend merely to the parts actually exposed to view. It cannot, however, be too forcibly impressed that the condition is universal in the body. If the lungs could be seen, they, too, would be found with their vessels injected; if the brain and spinal cord could be laid open to view, they would be discovered in the same condition; if the stomach, the liver, the spleen, the kidneys or any other vascular organs or parts could be exposed, the vascular engorgement would be equally manifest. In the lower animals, I have been able to witness this extreme vascular condition in the lungs, and there are here presented to you two drawings from nature, showing, one the lungs in a natural state of an animal killed by a sudden blow, the other the lungs of an animal killed equally suddenly, but at a time when it was under the influence of alcohol. You will see, as if you were looking at the structures themselves, how different they are in respect to the blood which they contained, how intensely charged with blood is the lung in which the vessels had been paralyzed by the alcoholic spirit.

EFFECT ON THE BRAIN.

"I once had the unusual, though unhappy, opportunity of observing the same phenomenon in the brain structure of a man, who, in a paroxysm of alcoholic excitement, decapitated himself under the wheel of a railway carriage, and whose brain was instantaneously evolved from the skull by the crash. The brain itself, entire, was before me within three minutes after the death. It exhaled the odor of spirit most distinctly, and its membranes and minute structures were vascular in the extreme. It looked as if it had been recently injected with vermilion. The white matter of the cerebrum, studded with red points, could scarcely be distinguished, when it was incised, by its natural whiteness; and the pia-mater, or internal vascular membrane covering the brain, resembled a delicate web of coagulated red blood, so tensely were its fine vessels engorged.

"I should add that this condition extended through both the larger and the smaller brain, the cerebrum and cerebellum, but was not so marked in the medulla or commencing portion of the spinal cord.

THE SPINAL CORD AND NERVES.

"The action of alcohol continued beyond the first stage, the function of the spinal cord is influenced. Through this part of the nervous system we are accustomed, in health, to perform automatic acts of a mechanical kind, which proceed systematically even when we are thinking or speaking on other subjects. Thus a skilled workman will continue his mechanical work perfectly, while his mind is bent on some other subject; and thus we all perform various acts in a purely automatic way, without calling in the aid of the higher centres, except something more than ordinary occurs to demand their service, upon which we think before we perform. Under alcohol, as the spinal centres become influenced, these pure automatic acts cease to be correctly carried on. That the hand may reach any object, or the foot be correctly planted, the higher intellectual centre must be invoked to make the proceeding secure. There follows quickly upon this a deficient power of co-ordination of muscular movement. The nervous control of certain of the muscles is lost, and the nervous stimulus is more or less enfeebled. The muscles of the lower lip in the human subject usually fail first of all, then the muscles of the lower limbs, and it is worthy of remark that the extensor muscles give way earlier than the flexors. The muscles themselves, by this time, are also failing in power; they respond more feebly than is natural to the nervous stimulus; they, too, are coming under the depressing influence of the paralyzing agent, their structure is temporarily deranged, and their contractile power reduced.

"This modification of the animal functions under alcohol, marks the second degree of its action. In young subjects, there is now, usually, vomiting with faintness, followed by gradual relief from the burden of the poison.

AN UTTER WRECK.

EFFECT ON THE BRAIN CENTRES.

"The alcoholic spirit carried yet a further degree, the cerebral or brain centres become influenced; they are reduced in power, and the controlling influences of will and of judgment are lost. As these centres are unbalanced and thrown into chaos, the rational part of the nature of the man gives way before the emotional, passional or organic part. The reason is now off duty, or is fooling with duty, and all the mere animal instincts and sentiments are laid atrociously bare. The coward shows up more craven, the braggart more boastful, the cruel more merciless, the untruthful more false, the carnal more degraded. '*In vino veritas*' expresses, even, indeed, to physiological accuracy, the true condition. The reason, the emotions, the instincts, are all in a state of carnival, and in chaotic feebleness.

"Finally, the action of the alcohol still extending, the superior brain centres are overpowered; the senses are beclouded, the voluntary muscular prostration is perfected, sensibility is lost, and the body lies a mere log, dead by all but one-fourth, on which alone its life hangs. The heart still remains true to its duty, and while it just lives it feeds the breathing power. And so the circulation and the respiration, in the otherwise inert mass, keeps the mass within the bare domain of life until the poison begins to pass away and the nervous centres to revive again. It is happy for the inebriate that, as a rule, the brain fails so long before the heart that he has neither the power nor the sense to continue his process of destruction up to the act of death of his circulation. Therefore he lives to die another day.

* * * * * * * *

"Such is an outline of the primary action of alcohol on those who may be said to be unaccustomed to it, or who have not yet fallen into a fixed habit of taking it. For a long time the organism will bear these perversions of its functions without apparent injury, but if the experiment be repeated too often and too long, if it be continued after the term of life when the body is fully developed, when the elasticity of the membranes and of the blood-vessels is lessened, and when the tone of the muscular fibre is reduced, then organic series of structural changes, so characteristic of the persistent effects of spirit, become prominent and permanent. Then the external surface becomes darkened and congested, its vessels, in parts, visibly large; the skin becomes blotched, the proverbial red nose is defined, and those other striking vascular changes which disfigure many who may probably be called moderate alcoholics, are developed. These changes, belonging, as they do, to external surfaces, come under direct observation; they are accompanied with certain other changes in the internal organs, which we shall show to be more destructive still."

CHAPTER III.

IT CURSES THE BODY.—Continued.

WE have quoted thus freely in the preceding chapter, in order that the intelligent and thoughtful reader, who is really seeking for the truth in regard to the physical action of alcohol, may be able to gain clear impressions on the subject. The specific changes wrought by this substance on the internal organs are of a most serious character, and should be well understood by all who indulge habitually in its use.

EFFECT ON THE MEMBRANES.

The parts which first suffer from alcohol are those expansions of the body which the anatomists call the membranes. "The skin is a membranous envelope. Through the whole of the alimentary surface, from the lips downward, and through the bronchial passages to their minutest ramifications, extends the mucous membrane. The lungs, the heart, the liver, the kidneys are folded in delicate membranes, which can be stripped easily from these parts. If you take a portion of bone, you will find it easy to strip off from it a membranous sheath or covering; if you examine a joint, you will find both the head and the socket lined with membranes. The whole of the intestines are enveloped in a fine membrane called *peritoneum.* All the muscles are enveloped in membranes, and the fasciculi, or bundles and fibres of muscles, have their membranous sheathing. The brain and spinal cord are enveloped in three membranes; one nearest to themselves, a pure vascular structure, a net-work of blood-vessels; another, a thin serous structure; a third, a strong fibrous structure. The eyeball is a structure of colloidal humors and membranes, and of nothing else. To complete the description, the minute structures of the vital organs are enrolled in membranous matter."

These membranes are the filters of the body. "In their absence there could be no building of structure, no solidification of tissue, nor organic mechanism. Passive themselves, they, nevertheless, separate all structures into their respective positions and adaptations."

MEMBRANOUS DETERIORATIONS.

In order to make perfectly clear to the reader's mind the action and use of these membranous expansions, and the way in which alcohol deteriorates them, and obstructs their work, we quote again from Dr. Richardson:

"The animal receives from the vegetable world and from the earth the food and drink it requires for its sustenance and motion. It receives colloidal food for its muscles; combustible food for its motion;

water for the solution of its various parts; salt for constructive and other physical purposes. These have all to be arranged in the body; and they are arranged by means of the membranous envelopes. Through these membranes nothing can pass that is not, for the time, in a state of aqueous solution, like water or soluble salts. Water passes freely through them, salts pass freely through them, but the constructive matter of the active parts that is colloidal does not pass; it is retained in them until it is chemically decomposed into the soluble type of matter. When we take for our food a portion of animal flesh, it is first resolved, in digestion, into a soluble fluid before it can be absorbed; in the blood it is resolved into the fluid colloidal condition; in the solids it is laid down within the membranes into new structure, and when it has played its part, it is digested again, if I may so say, into a crystalloidal soluble substance, ready to be carried away and replaced by addition of new matter, then it is dialysed or passed through the membranes into the blood, and is disposed of in the excretions.

"See, then, what an all-important part these membranous structures play in the animal life. Upon their integrity all the silent work of the building up of the body depends. If these membranes are rendered too porous, and let out the colloidal fluids of the blood—the albumen, for example —the body so circumstanced, dies; dies as if it were slowly bled to death. If, on the contrary, they become condensed or thickened, or loaded with foreign material, then they fail to allow the natural fluids to pass through them. They fail to dialyse, and the result is, either an accumulation of the fluid in a closed cavity, or contraction of the substance inclosed within the membrane, or dryness of membrane in surfaces that ought to be freely lubricated and kept apart. In old age we see the effects of modification of membrane naturally induced; we see the fixed joint, the shrunken and feeble muscle, the dimmed eye, the deaf ear, the enfeebled nervous function.

"It may possibly seem, at first sight, that I am leading immediately away from the subject of the secondary action of alcohol. It is not so. I am leading directly to it. Upon all these membranous structures alcohol exerts a direct perversion of action. It produces in them a thickening, a shrinking and an inactivity that reduces their functional power. That they may work rapidly and equally, they require to be at all times charged with water to saturation. If, into contact with them, any agent is brought that deprives them of water, then is their work interfered with; they cease to separate the saline constituents properly; and, if the evil that is thus started, be allowed to continue, they contract upon their contained matter in whatever organ it may be situated, and condense it.

"In brief, under the prolonged influence of alcohol those changes which take place from it in the blood corpuscles, and which have already been described, extend to the other organic parts, involving them in structural deteriorations, which are always dangerous, and are often ultimately fatal."

ACTION OF ALCOHOL ON THE STOMACH.

Passing from the effect of alcohol upon the membranes, we come to its action on the stomach. That it impairs, instead of assisting digestion, has already been shown in the extract from Dr. Monroe, given near the commencement of the preceding chapter. A large amount of medical testimony could be quoted in corroboration, but enough has been educed. We shall only quote Dr. Richardson on "Alcoholic Dyspepsia:"

"The stomach, unable to produce, in proper quantity, the natural digestive fluid, and also unable to absorb the food which it may imperfectly digest, is in constant anxiety and irritation. It is oppressed with the sense of nausea; it is oppressed with the sense of emptiness and prostration; it is oppressed with a sense of distention; it is oppressed with a loathing for food, and it is teased with a craving for more drink. Thus there is engendered a permanent disorder which, for politeness' sake, is called dyspepsia, and for which different remedies are often sought but never found. Antibilious pills—whatever they may mean—Seidlitz powders, effervescing waters, and all that pharmacopœia of aids to further indigestion, in which the afflicted who nurse their own diseases so liberally and innocently indulge, are tried in vain. I do not strain a syllable when I state that the worst forms of confirmed indigestion originate in the practice that is here explained. By this practice all the functions are vitiated, the skin at one moment is flushed and perspiring, and at the next moment it is pale, cold and clammy, while every other secreting structure is equally disarranged."

TIC-DOULOUREUX AND SCIATICA.

Nervous derangements follow as a matter of course, for the delicate membranes which envelope and immediately surround the nervous cords, are affected by the alcohol more readily than the coarser membranous textures of other parts of the body, and give rise to a series of troublesome conditions, which are too often attributed to other than the true causes. Some of these are thus described: "The perverted condition of the membranous covering of the nerves gives rise to pressure within the sheath of the nerve, and to pain as a consequence. To the pain thus excited the term neuralgia is commonly applied, or "tic;" or, if the large nerve running down the thigh be the seat of the pain, 'sciatica.' Sometimes this pain is developed as a toothache. It is pain commencing, in nearly every instance, at some point where a nerve is inclosed in a bony cavity, or where pressure is easily excited, as at the lower jawbone near the centre of the chin, or at the opening in front of the lower part of the ear, or at the opening over the eyeball in the frontal bone."

DEGENERATION OF THE LIVER.

The organic deteriorations which follow the long-continued use of alcoholic drinks are often of a serious and fatal character. The same author says: "The organ of the body, that, perhaps, the most frequently undergoes structural changes from alcohol, is the *liver*. The capacity of this organ for holding active substances in its cellular parts, is one of its marked physiological distinctions. In instances of poisoning by arsenic, antimony, strychnine and other poisonous compounds, we turn to the liver, in conducting our analyses, as if it were the central depot of the foreign matter. It is, practically, the same in respect to alcohol. The liver of the confirmed alcoholic is, probably, never free from the influence of the poison; it is too often saturated with it. The effect of the alcohol upon the liver is upon the minute membranous or capsular structure of the organ, upon which it acts to prevent the proper dialysis and free secretion. The organ, at first, becomes large from the distention of its vessels, the surcharge of fluid matter and the thickening of tissue. After a time, there follows contraction of membrane, and slow shrinking of the whole mass of the organ in its cellular parts. Then the shrunken, hardened, roughened mass is said to be 'hob-nailed,' a common, but expressive term. By the time this change occurs, the body of him in whom it is developed is usually dropsical in its lower parts, owing to the obstruction offered to the returning blood by the veins, and his fate is sealed. * * * Again, under an increase of fatty substance in the body, the structure of the liver may be charged with fatty cells, and undergo what is technically designated fatty degeneration."

HOW THE KIDNEYS SUFFER.

"The kidneys, also, suffer deterioration. Their minute structures undergo fatty modification; their vessels lose their due elasticity of power of contraction; or their membranes permit to pass through them the albumen from the blood. This last condition reached, the body loses power as if it were being gradually drained even of its blood.

CONGESTION OF THE LUNGS.

"The vessels of the lungs are easily relaxed by alcohol; and as they, of all parts, are most exposed to vicissitudes of heat and cold, they are readily congested when, paralyzed by the spirit, they are subjected to the effects of a sudden fall of atmospheric temperature. Thus, the suddenly fatal congestions of lungs which so easily befall the confirmed alcoholic during the severe winter seasons."

ORGANIC DETERIORATIONS OF THE HEART.

The heart is one of the greatest sufferers from alcohol. Quoting again from Dr. Richardson:

"The membranous structures which envelope and line the organ are changed in quality, are thickened, rendered cartilaginous, and even calcareous or bony.

Then the valves, which are made up of folds of membrane, lose their suppleness, and what is called valvular disease is permanently established. The coats of the great blood-vessel leading from the heart, the aorto, share, not unfrequently, in the same changes of structure, so that the vessel loses its elasticity and its power to feed the heart by the recoil from its distention, after the heart, by its stroke, has filled it with blood.

"Again, the muscular structure of the heart fails, owing to degenerative changes in its tissue. The elements of the muscular fibre are replaced by fatty cells; or, if not so replaced, are themselves transferred into a modified muscular texture in which the power of contraction is greatly reduced.

"Those who suffer from these organic deteriorations of the central and governing organ of the circulation of the blood learn the fact so insidiously, it hardly breaks upon them until the mischief is far advanced. They are, for years, conscious of a central failure of power from slight causes, such as overexertion, trouble, broken rest, or too long abstinence from food. They feel what they call a 'sinking,' but they know that wine or some other stimulant will at once relieve the sensation. Thus they seek to relieve it until at last they discover that the remedy fails. The jaded, overworked, faithful heart will bear no more; it has run its course, and, the governor of the blood-streams broken, the current either overflows into the tissues, gradually damming up the courses, or under some slight shock or excess of motion, ceases wholly at the centre."

EPILEPSY AND PARALYSIS.

Lastly, the brain and spinal cord, and all the nervous matter, become, under the influence of alcohol, subject alike to organic deterioration "The membranes enveloping the nervous substance undergo thickening; the blood-vessels are subjected to change of structure, by which their resistance and resiliency is impaired; and the true nervous matter is sometimes modified, by softening or shrinking of its texture, by degeneration of its cellular structure or by interposition of fatty particles. These deteriorations of cerebral and spinal matter give rise to a series of derangements, which show themselves in the worst forms of nervous diseases—epilepsy; paralysis, local or general; insanity."

We have quoted thus largely from Dr. Richardson's valuable lectures, in order that our readers may have an intelligent comprehension of this most important subject. It is because the great mass of the people are ignorant of the real character of the effects produced on the body by alcohol that so many indulge in its use, and lay the foundation for troublesome, and often painful and fatal diseases in their later years.

In corroboration of Dr. Richardson's testimony against alcohol, we will, in closing this chapter, make a few quotations from other medical authorities.

FARTHER MEDICAL TESTIMONY.

Dr. Ezra M. Hunt says: "The capacity of the alcohols for impairment of functions and the initiation and promotion of organic lesions in vital parts, is unsurpassed by any record in the whole range of medicine. *The facts as to this are so indisputable, and so far granted by the profession, as to be no longer debatable.* Changes in stomach and liver, in kidneys and lungs, in the blood-vessels to the minutest capillary, and in the blood to the smallest red and white blood disc disturbances of secretion, fibroid and fatty degenerations in almost every organ, impairment of muscular power, impressions so profound on both nervous systems as to be often toxic—these, and such as these, are the oft manifested results. And these are not confined to those called intemperate."

Professor Youmans says: "It is evident that, so far from being the conservator of health, alcohol is an active and powerful cause of disease, interfering, as it does, with the respiration, the circulation and the nutrition; now, is any other result possible?"

Dr. F. R. Lees says: "That alcohol should contribute to the fattening process under certain conditions, and produce in drinkers fatty degeneration of the blood, follows, as a matter of course, since, on the one hand, we have an agent that *retains waste* matter by lowering the nutritive and excretory functions, and on the other, a *direct poisoner* of the vesicles of the vital stream."

Dr. Henry Monroe says: "There is no kind of tissue, whether healthy or morbid, that may not undergo fatty degeneration; and there is no organic disease so troublesome to the medical man, or so difficult of cure. If, by the aid of the miscroscope, we examine a very fine section of muscle taken from a person in good health, we find the muscles firm, elastic and of a bright red color, made up of parallel fibres, with beautiful crossings or striæ; but, if we similarly examine the muscle of a man who leads an idle, sedentary life, and indulges in intoxicating drinks, we detect, at once, a pale, flabby, inelastic, oily appearance. Alcoholic narcotization appears to produce this peculiar conditions of the tissues *more than any other agent with which we are acquainted.* 'Three-quarters of the chronic illness which the medical man has to treat,' says Dr. Chambers, 'are occasioned by this disease.' The eminent French analytical chemist, Lecanu, found as much as one hundred and seventeen parts of fat in one thousand parts of a drunkard's blood, the highest estimate of the quantity in health being eight and one-quarter parts, while the ordinary quantity is not more than two or three parts, so that the blood of the drunkard contains forty times in excess of the ordinary quantity."

Dr. Hammond, who has written, in partial defense of alcohol as containing a food power, says: "When I say that it, of all other causes, *is most prolific* in exciting derangements of the brain, the spinal cord and the nerves, I make a statement which my own experience shows to be correct."

Another eminent physician says of alcohol: "It substitutes suppuration for growth. * * It helps time to produce the effects of age; and, in a word, is the genius of degeneration."

Dr. Monroe, from whom we have already quoted, says: "Alcohol, taken in small quantities, or largely diluted, as in the form of beer, causes the stomach gradually to lose its tone, and makes it dependent upon artificial stimulus. Atony, or want of tone of the stomach, gradually supervenes, and incurable disorder of health results. * * * Should a dose of alcoholic drink be taken daily, the heart will very often become hypertrophied, or enlarged throughout. Indeed, it is painful to witness how *many* persons are actually laboring under disease of the heart, owing chiefly to the use of alcoholic liquors."

Dr. T. K. Chambers, physician to the Prince of Wales, says: "Alcohol is really the most ungenerous diet there is. It impoverishes the blood, and there is no surer road to that degeneration of muscular fibre so much to be feared; and in heart disease it is more especially hurtful, by quickening the beat, causing capillary congestion and irregular circulation, and thus mechanically inducing dilatation.'

Sir Henry Thompson, a distinguished surgeon, says: "Don't take your daily wine under any pretext of its doing you good. Take it frankly as a luxury— one which must be paid for, by some persons very lightly, by some at a high price, *but always to be paid for.* And, mostly, some loss of health, or of mental power, or of calmness of temper, or of judgment, is the price."

Dr. Charles Jewett says: "The late Prof. Parks, of England, in his great work on Hygiene, has effectually disposed of the notion, long and very generally entertained, that alcohol is a valuable prophylactic where a bad climate, bad water and other conditions unfavorable to health exist; and an unfortunate experiment with the article, in the Union army, on the banks of the Chickahominy, in the year 1863, proved conclusively that, instead of guarding the human constitution against the influence of agencies hostile to health, its use gives to them additional force. The medical history of the British army in India teaches the same lesson."

But why present farther testimony? Is not the evidence complete? To the man who values good health; who would not lay the foundation for disease and suffering in his later years, we need not offer a single additional argument in favor of entire abstinence from alcoholic drinks. He will eschew them as poisons.

CHAPTER IV.

IT CURSES THE SOUL.

THE physical disasters that follow the continued use of intoxicating beverages are sad enough, and terrible enough; but the surely attendant mental, moral and spiritual disasters are sadder and more terrible still. If you disturb the healthy condition of the brain, which is the physical organ through which the mind acts, you disturb the mind. It will not have the same clearness of perception as before; nor have the same rational control over the impulses and passions.

In what manner alcohol deteriorates the body and brain has been shown in the two preceding chapters. In this one we purpose showing how the curse goes deeper than the body and brain, and involves the whole man—morally and spiritually, as well as physically.

HEAVENLY ORDER IN THE BODY.

In order to understand a subject clearly, certain general laws, or principles, must be seen and admitted. And here we assume, as a general truth, that health in the human body is normal heavenly order on the physical plane of life, and that any disturbance of that order exposes the man to destructive influences, which are evil and infernal in their character Above the natural and physical plane, and resting upon it, while man lives in this world, is the mental and spiritual plane, or degree of life. This degree is in heavenly order when the reason is clear, and the appetites and passions under its wise control. But, if, through any cause, this fine equipoise is disturbed, or lost, then a way is opened for the influx of more subtle evil influences than such as invade the body, because they have power to act upon the reason and the passions, obscuring the one and inflaming the others.

MENTAL DISTURBANCES.

We know how surely the loss of bodily health results in mental disturbance. If the seat of disease be remote from the brain, the disturbance is usually slight; but it increases as the trouble comes nearer and nearer to that organ, and shows itself in multiform ways according to character, temperament or inherited disposition; but almost always in a predominance of what is evil instead of good. There will be fretfulness, or ill-nature, or selfish exactions, or mental obscurity, or unreasoning demands, or, it may be, vicious and cruel propensities, where, when the brain was undisturbed by disease, reason held rule with patience and loving kindness. If the disease which has attacked the brain goes on increasing, the mental disease which follows as a consequence of organic disturbance or deterioration, will have increased also, until insanity may be established in some one or more of its many sad and varied forms.

INSANITY.

It is, therefore, a very serious thing for a man to take into his body any substance which, on reaching that wonderfully delicate organ—the brain, sets up therein a diseased action; for, diseased mental action is sure to follow, and there is only one true name for mental disease, and that is *insanity*. A fever is a fever, whether it be light or intensely burning; and so any disturbance of the mind's rational equipoise is insanity, whether it be in the simplest form of temporary obscurity, or in the midnight of a totally darkened intellect.

We are not writing in the interest of any special theory, nor in the spirit of partisanship; but with an earnest desire to make the truth appear. The reader must not accept anything simply because we say it, but because he sees it to be true. Now, as to this matter of insanity, let him think calmly. The word is one that gives us a shock; and, as we hear it, we almost involuntarily thank God for the good gift of a well-balanced mind. What, if from any cause this beautiful equipoise should be disturbed and the mind lose its power to think clearly, or to hold the lower passions in due control? Shall we exceed the truth if we say that the man in whom this takes place is insane just in the degree that he has lost his rational self-control; and that he is restored when he regains that control?

In this view, the question as to the hurtfulness of alcoholic drinks assumes a new and graver aspect. Do they disturb the brain when they come in contact with its substance; and deteriorate it if the contact be long continued? Fact, observation, experience and scientific investigation all emphatically say yes; and we know that if the brain be disordered the mind will be disordered, likewise; and a disordered mind is an insane mind. Clearly, then, in the degree that a man impairs or hurts his brain—temporarily or continuously—in that degree his mind is unbalanced; in that degree he is not a truly rational and sane man.

We are holding the reader's thought just here that he may have time to think, and to look at the question in the light of reason and common sense. So far as he does this, will he be able to feel the force of such evidence as we shall educe in what follows, and to comprehend its true meaning.

NO SUBSTANCE AFFECTS THE BRAIN LIKE ALCOHOL.

Other substances besides alcohol act injuriously on the brain; but there is none that compares with this in the extent, variety and diabolical aspect of the mental aberrations which follow its use. We are not speaking thoughtlessly or wildly; but simply uttering a truth well-known to every man of observation, and which every man, and especially those who take this substance in any form, should lay deeply to heart. Why it is that such awful and destructive forms of insanity should follow, as they do, the use of alcohol it is not for us to say. That they do follow it, we know, and we hold up the fact in solemn warning.

INHERITED LATENT EVIL FORCES.

Another consideration, which should have weight with every one, is this, that no man can tell what may be the character of the legacy he has received from his ancestors. He may have an inheritance of latent evil forces, transmitted through many generations, which only await some favoring opportunity to spring into life and action. So long as he maintains a rational self-control, and the healthy order of his life be not disturbed, they may continue quiescent; but if his brain loses its equipoise, or is hurt or impaired, then a diseased psychical condition may be induced and the latent evil forces be quickened into life.

No substance in nature, as far as yet known, has, when it reaches the brain, such power to induce

MENTAL AND MORAL CHANGES OF A DISASTROUS CHARACTER

as alcohol. Its transforming power is marvelous, and often appalling. It seems to open a way of entrance into the soul for all classes of foolish, insane or malignant spirits, who, so long as it remains in contact with the brain, are able to hold possession.

Men of the kindest nature when sober, act often like fiends when drunk. Crimes and outrages are committed, which shock and shame the perpetrators when the excitement of inebriation has passed away. Referring to this subject, Dr. Henry Munroe says:

"It appears from the experience of Mr. Fletcher, who has paid much attention to the cases of drunkards, from the remarks of Mr. Dunn, in his 'Medical Psychology,' and from observations of my own, that there is some analogy between our physical and psychical natures; for, as the physical part of us, when its power is at a low ebb, becomes susceptible of morbid influences which, in full vigor, would pass over it without effect, so when the psychical (synonymous with the *moral*) part of the brain has its healthy function disturbed and deranged by the introduction of a morbid poison like alcohol, the individual so circumstanced sinks in depravity, and

BECOMES THE HELPLESS SUBJECT OF THE FORCES OF EVIL,

which are powerless against a nature free from the morbid influences of alcohol.

"Different persons are affected in different ways by the same poison. Indulgence in alcoholic drinks may act upon one or more of the cerebral organs; and, as its necessary consequence, the manifestations of functional disturbance will follow in such of the mental powers as these organs subserve. If the indulgence be continued, then, either from deranged nutrition or organic lesion, manifestations formerly

"TAKE WARNING BY MY CAREER."

developed only during a fit of intoxication may become *permanent*, and terminate in insanity or dypsomania. M. Flourens first pointed out the fact that certain morbific agents, when introduced into the current of the circulation, tend to act *primarily* and *specially* on one nervous centre in preference to that of another, by virtue of some special elective affinity between such morbific agents and certain ganglia. Thus, in the tottering gait of the tipsy man, we see the influence of alcohol upon the functions of the *cerebellum* in the impairment of its power of co-ordinating the muscles.

"Certain writers on diseases of the mind make especial allusion to that form of insanity termed DYPSOMANIA, in which a person has an unquenchable thirst for alcoholic drinks—a tendency as decidedly maniacal as that of *homicidal mania;* or the uncontrollable desire to burn, termed *pyromania;* or to steal, called *kleptomania.*

HOMICIDAL MANIA.

"The different tendencies of homicidal mania in different individuals are often only nursed into action when the current of the blood has been poisoned with alcohol. I had a case of a person who, whenever his brain was so excited, told me that he experienced a most uncontrollable desire to kill or injure some one; so much so, that he could at times hardly restrain himself from the action, and was obliged to refrain from all stimulants, lest, in an unlucky moment, he might commit himself. Townley, who murdered the young lady of his affections, for which he was sentenced to be imprisoned in a lunatic asylum for life, *poisoned his brain with brandy* and soda-water before he committed the rash act. The brandy stimulated into action certain portions of the brain, which acquired such a power as to subjugate his will, and hurry him to the performance of a frightful deed, opposed alike to his better judgment and his ordinary desires.

"As to *pyromania*, some years ago I knew a laboring man in a country village, who, whenever he had had a few glasses of ale at the public-house, would chuckle with delight at the thought of firing certain gentlemen's stacks. Yet, when his brain was free from the poison, a quieter, better-disposed man could not be. Unfortunately, he became addicted to habits of intoxication; and, one night, under alcoholic excitement, fired some stacks belonging to his employers, for which he was sentenced for fifteen years to a penal settlement, where his brain would never again be alcoholically excited.

KLEPTOMANIA.

"Next, I will give an example of *kleptomania*. I knew, many years ago, a very clever, industrious and talented young man, who told me that whenever he had been drinking, he could hardly withstand the temptation of stealing anything that came in his way; but that these feelings never troubled him at other times. One afternoon, after he had been indulging with his fellow-workmen in drink, his will, unfortunately, was overpowered, and he took from the mansion where he was working some articles of worth, for which he was accused, and afterwards sentenced to a term of imprisonment. When set at liberty he had the good fortune to be placed among some kind-hearted persons, vulgarly called *teetotallers;* and, from conscientious motives, signed the PLEDGE, now above twenty years ago. From that time to the present moment he has never experienced the overmastering desire which so often beset him in his drinking days—to take that which was not his own. Moreover, no pretext on earth could now entice him to taste of any liquor containing alcohol, feeling that, under its influence, he might again fall its victim. He holds an influential position in the town where he resides.

"I have known some ladies of good position in society, who, after a dinner or supper-party, and after having taken sundry glasses of wine, could not withstand the temptation of taking home any little article not their own, when the opportunity offered; and who, in their sober moments, have returned them, as if taken by mistake. We have many instances recorded in our police reports of gentlemen of position, under the influence of drink, committing thefts of the most paltry articles, afterwards returned to the owners by their friends, which can only be accounted for, psychologically, by the fact that the *will* had been for the time completely overpowered by the subtle influence of alcohol.

LOSS OF MENTAL CLEARNESS.

"That alcohol, whether taken in large or small doses, immediately disturbs the natural functions of the mind and body, is now conceded by the most eminent physiologists. Dr. Brinton says: 'Mental acuteness, accuracy of conception, and delicacy of the senses, are all so far opposed by the action of alcohol, as that the maximum efforts of each are *incompatible* with the ingestion of any moderate quantity of fermented liquid. Indeed, there is scarcely any calling which demands skillful and exact effort of mind and body, or which requires the balanced exercise of many faculties, that does not illustrate this rule. The mathematician, the gambler, the metaphysician, the billiard-player, the author, the artist, the physician, would, if they could analyze their experience aright, generally concur in the statement, that *a single glass will often suffice to take*, so to speak, *the edge off both mind and body*, and to reduce their capacity to something below what is relatively their perfection of work.'

"Not long ago, a railway train was driven carelessly into one of the principal London stations, running into another train, killing, by the collision, six or seven persons, and injuring many others. From the evidence at the inquest, it appeared that the guard was reckoned sober, *only he had had two glasses of ale* with a friend at a previous station. Now, reasoning psychologically, these two glasses of ale had probably been instrumental in *taking off the edge* from his perceptions and prudence, and producing a carelessness or boldness of action which would not have occurred under the cooling, temperate influence of a beverage free from alcohol. Many persons have admitted to me that they were not the same after taking even one glass of ale or wine that they were before, and could not *thoroughly* trust themselves after they had taken this single glass."

IMPAIRMENT OF MEMORY.

An impairment of the memory is among the early symptoms of alcoholic derangement.

"This," says Dr. Richardson, "extends even to forgetfulness of the commonest things; to names of familiar persons, to dates, to duties of daily life. Strangely, too," he adds, "this failure, like that which indicates, in the aged, the era of second childishness and mere oblivion, does not extend to the things of the past, but is confined to events that are passing. On old memories the mind retains its power; on new ones it requires constant prompting and sustainment."

In this failure of memory nature gives a solemn warning that imminent peril is at hand. Well for the habitual drinker if he heed the warning. Should he not do so, symptoms of a more serious character will, in time, develop themselves, as the brain becomes more and more diseased, ending, it may be, in permanent insanity.

MENTAL AND MORAL DISEASES.

Of the mental and moral diseases which too often follow the regular drinking of alcohol, we have painful records in asylum reports, in medical testimony and in our daily observation and experience. These are so full and varied, and thrust so constantly on our attention, that the wonder is that men are not afraid to run the terrible risks involved even in what is called the moderate use of alcoholic beverages.

In 1872, a select committee of the House of Commons, appointed "to consider the best plan for the control and management of habitual drunkards," called upon some of the most eminent medical men in Great Britain to give their testimony in answer to a large number of questions, embracing every topic within the range of inquiry, from the pathology of inebriation to the practical usefulness of prohibitory laws. In this testimony much was said about the effect of alcoholic stimulation on the mental condition and moral character. One physician, Dr. James Crichton Brown, who, in ten years' experience as superintendent of lunatic asylums, has paid special attention to the relations of habitual drunkenness to insanity, having carefully examined five hundred cases, testified that alcohol, taken in excess, produced different forms of mental disease, of which he mentioned four classes: 1. *Mania a potu*, or alcoholic mania. 2. The monomania of suspicion. 3. Chronic alcoholism, characterized by failure of the memory and power of judgment, with partial paralysis —generally ending fatally. 4. Dypsomania, or an *irresistible* craving for alcoholic stimulants, occurring very frequently, paroxysmally, and with constant liability to periodical exacerbations, when the craving becomes altogether uncontrollable. Of this latter form of disease, he says: "This is invariably associated with a certain *impairment of the intellect, and of the affections and the moral powers.*"

Dr. Alexander Peddie, a physician of over thirty-seven years' practice in Edinburgh, gave, in his evidence, many remarkable instances of the moral perversions that followed continued drinking.

RELATION BETWEEN INSANITY AND DRUNKENNESS.

Dr. John Nugent said that his experience of twenty-six years among lunatics, led him to believe that there is a very close relation between the results of the abuse of alcohol and insanity. The population of Ireland had decreased, he said, two millions in twenty-five years, but there was the same amount of insanity now that there was before. He attributed this, in a great measure, to indulgence in drink.

Dr. Arthur Mitchell, Commissioner of Lunacy for Scotland, testified that the excessive use of alcohol caused a large amount of the lunacy, crime and pauperism of that country. In some men, he said, habitual drinking leads to other diseases than insanity, because the effect is always in the direction of the proclivity, but it is certain that there are many in whom there is a clear proclivity to insanity, *who would escape that dreadful consummation but for drinking; excessive drinking in many persons determining the insanity to which they are, at any rate, predisposed.* The children of drunkards, he further said, are in a larger proportion idiotic than other children, and in a larger proportion become themselves drunkards; they are also in a larger proportion liable to the ordinary forms of acquired insanity.

Dr. Winslow Forbes believed that in the habitual drunkard the whole nervous structure, and the brain especially, became poisoned by alcohol. All the mental symptoms which you see accompanying ordinary intoxication, he remarks, result from the poisonous effects of alcohol on the brain. It is the brain which is mainly effected. In temporary drunkenness, the brain becomes in an abnormal state of alimentation, and if this habit is persisted in for years, the nervous tissue itself becomes permeated with alcohol, and organic changes take place in the nervous tissues of the brain, producing *that frightful and dreadful chronic insanity which we see in lunatic asylums, traceable entirely to habits of intoxication.* A large percentage of frightful mental and brain disturbances can, he declared, be traced to the drunkenness of parents.

Dr. D. G. Dodge, late of the New York State Inebriate Asylum, who, with Dr. Joseph Parrish, gave testimony before the committee of the House of Commons, said, in one of his answers: "With the excessive use of alcohol, functional disorder will invariably appear, and no organ will be more seriously affected, and possibly impaired, than the brain. *This is shown in the inebriate by a weakened intellect, a general debility of the mental faculties*, a partial or total loss of self-respect, and a departure of the power of self-command; all of which, acting together, place the victim at the mercy of a depraved and morbid appetite, and make him utterly powerless, by his own unaided efforts, to secure his recovery from the disease which is destroying him." And he adds: "I am of opinion that there is a

GREAT SIMILARITY BETWEEN INEBRIETY AND INSANITY.

I am decidedly of opinion that the former has taken its place in the family of diseases as prominently as its twin-brother insanity; and, in my opinion, the day is not far distant when the pathology of the former will be as fully understood and as successfully treated as the latter, and even more successfully, since it is more within the reach and bounds of human control, which, wisely exercised and scientifically administered, may prevent curable inebriation from verging into possible incurable insanity."

GENERAL IMPAIRMENT OF THE FACULTIES.

In a more recent lecture than the one from which we have quoted so freely, Dr. Richardson, speaking of the action of alcohol on the mind, gives the following sad picture of its ravages:

"An analysis of the condition of the mind induced and maintained by the free daily use of alcohol as a drink, reveals a singular order of facts. The manifestation fails altogether to reveal the exaltation of any reasoning power in a useful or satisfactory direction. I have never met with an instance in which such a claim for alcohol has been made. On the contrary, confirmed alcoholics constantly say that for this or that work, requiring thought and attention, it is necessary to forego some of the usual potations in order to have a cool head for hard work.

"On the other side, the experience is overwhelmingly in favor of the observation that the use of

ALCOHOL SELLS THE REASONING POWERS,

make weak men and women the easy prey of the wicked and strong, and leads men and women who should know better into every grade of misery and vice. * * * If, then, alcohol enfeebles the reason, what part of the mental constitution does it exalt and excite? It excites and exalts those animal, organic, emotional centres of mind which, in the dual nature of man, so often cross and oppose that pure and abstract reasoning nature which lifts man above the lower animals, and rightly exercised, little lower than the angels.

IT EXCITES MAN'S WORST PASSIONS.

"Exciting these animal centres, it lets loose all the passions, and gives them more or less of unlicensed dominion over the man. It excites anger, and when it does not lead to this extreme, it keeps the mind fretful, irritable, dissatisfied and captious. * * * And if I were to take you through all the passions, love, hate, lust, envy, avarice and pride, I should but show you that alcohol ministers to them all; that, paralyzing the reason, it takes from off these passions that fine adjustment of reason, which places man above the lower animals. From the beginning to the end of its influence it subdues reason and sets the passions free. The analogies, physical and mental, are perfect. That which loosens the tension of the vessels which feed the body with due order and precision, and, thereby, lets loose the heart to violent excess and unbridled motion, loosens, also, the reason and lets loose the passion. In both instances, heart and head are, for a time, out of harmony; their balance broken. The man descends closer and closer to the lower animals. From the angels he glides farther and farther away.

A SAD AND TERRIBLE PICTURE.

"The *destructive* effects of alcohol on the human mind present, finally, the saddest picture of its influence. The most æsthetic artist can find no angel here. All is animal, and animal of the worst type. Memory irretrievably lost, words and very elements of speech forgotten or words displaced to have no meaning in them. Rage and anger persistent and mischievous, or remittent and impotent. Fear at every corner of life, distrust on every side, grief merged into blank despair, hopelessness into permanent melancholy. Surely no Pandemonium that ever poet dreamt of could equal that which would exist if all the drunkards of the world were driven into one mortal sphere.

"As I have moved among those who are physically stricken with alcohol, and have detected under the various disguises of name the fatal diseases, the pains and penalties it imposes on the body, the picture has been sufficiently cruel. But even that picture pales, as I conjure up, without any stretch of imagination, the devastations which the same agent inflicts on the mind. Forty per cent., the learned Superintendent of Colney Hatch, Dr. Sheppard, tells us, of those who were brought into that asylum in 1876, were so brought because of the direct or indirect effects of alcohol. If the facts of all the asylums were collected with equal care, the same tale would, I fear, be told. What need we further to show the destructive action on the human mind? The Pandemonium of drunkards; the grand transformation scene of that pantomime of drink which commences with moderation! Let it never more be

CRAZED BY DRINK.

"God's rational offspring . . . become a brute."

forgotten by those who love their fellow-men until, through their efforts, it is closed forever."

We might go on, adding page after page of evidence, showing how alcohol curses the souls, as well as the bodies, of men; but enough has been educed to force conviction on the mind of every reader not already satisfied of its poisonous and destructive quality.

How light are all evils flowing from intemperance compared with those which it thus inflicts on man's higher nature. "What," says Dr. W. E. Channing, "is the great essential evil of intemperance? The reply is given, when I say, that intemperance is the

VOLUNTARY EXTINCTION OF REASON.

The great evil is inward or spiritual. The intemperate man divests himself, for a time, of his rational and moral nature, casts from himself self-consciousness and self-command, brings on frenzy, and by repetition of this insanity, prostrates more and more his rational and moral powers. He sins immediately and directly against the rational nature, that Divine principle which distinguishes between truth and falsehood, between right and wrong action, which distinguishes man from the brute. This is the essence of the vice, what constitutes its peculiar guilt and woe, and what should particularly impress and awaken those who are laboring for its suppression. Other evils of intemperance are light compared with this, and almost all flow from this; and it is right, it is to be desired that all other evils should be joined with and follow this. It is to be desired, when a man lifts a suicidal arm against his higher life, when he quenches reason and conscience, that he and all others should receive solemn, startling warning of the greatness of his guilt; that terrible outward calamities should bear witness to the inward ruin which he is working; that the handwriting of judgment and woe on his countenance, form and whole condition, should declare what a fearful thing it is for a man, "God's rational offspring, to renounce his reason, and become a brute."

CHAPTER V.

NOT A FOOD, AND VERY LIMITED IN ITS RANGE AS A MEDICINE.

THE use of alcohol as a medicine has been very large. If his patient was weak and nervous, the physician too often ordered wine or ale; or, not taking the trouble to refer his own case to a physician, the invalid prescribed these articles for himself. If there was a failure of appetite, its restoration was sought in the use of one or both of the above-named forms of alcohol; or, perhaps, adopting a more heroic treatment, the sufferer poured brandy or whisky into his weak and sensitive stomach. Protection from cold was sought in a draught of some alcoholic beverage, and relief from fatigue and exhaustion in the use of the same deleterious substance. Indeed, there is scarcely any form of bodily ailment or discomfort, or mental disturbance, for the relief of which a resort was not had to alcohol in some one of its many forms.

It is fair to say that, as a medicine, its consumption has far exceeded that of any other substance prescribed and taken for physical and mental derangements.

The inquiry, then, as to the true remedial value

of alcohol is one of the gravest import; and it is of interest to know that for some years past the medical profession has been giving this subject a careful and thorough investigation. The result is to be found in the brief declaration made by the Section on Medicine, of the

INTERNATIONAL MEDICAL CONGRESS,

which met in Philadelphia in 1876. This body was composed of about six hundred delegates, from Europe and America, among them, some of the ablest men in the profession. Realizing the importance of some expression in relation to the use of alcohol, medical and otherwise, from this Congress, the National Temperance Society laid before it, through its President, W. E. Dodge, and Secretary, J. N. Stearns, the following memorial:

"The National Temperance Society sends greeting, and respectfully invites from your distinguished body a public declaration to the effect that alcohol should be classed with other powerful drugs; that, when prescribed medicinally, it should be with conscientious caution and a sense of grave responsibility; that it is in no sense food to the human system; that its improper use is productive of a large amount of physical disease, tending to deteriorate the human race; and to recommend, as representatives of enlightened science, to your several nationalities, total abstinence from alcoholic beverages."

In response to this memorial, the president of

the society received from J. Ewing Mears, M. D., Secretary of the Section on Medicine, International Congress, the following official letter, under date of September 9th, 1876:

"DEAR SIR: I am instructed by the Section on Medicine, International Medical Congress, of 1876, to transmit to you, as the action of the Section, the following conclusions adopted by it with regard to the use of alcohol in medicine, the same being in reply to the communication sent by the National Temperance Society.

"1. Alcohol is not shown to have a definite food value by any of the usual methods of chemical analysis or physiological investigation.

"2. Its use as a medicine is chiefly that of a cardiac stimulant, and often admits of substitution.

"3. As a medicine, it is not well fitted for self-prescription by the laity, and the medical profession is not accountable for such administration, or for the enormous evils arising therefrom.

"4. The purity of alcoholic liquors is, in general, not as well assured as that of articles used for medicine should be. The various mixtures, when used as medicine, should have definite and known composition, and should not be interchanged promiscuously."

The reader will see in this no hesitating or half-way speech. The declaration is strong and clear, that, as a food, alcohol is not shown, when subjected to the usual method of chemical or physiological investigation, to have any food value; and that, as a medicine, its use is chiefly confined to a cardiac stimulant, and often admits of substitution.

A declaration like this, coming, as it does, from a body of medical men representing the most advanced ideas held by the profession, must have great weight with the people. But we do not propose resting on this declaration alone. As it was based on the results of chemical and physiological investigations, let us go back of the opinion expressed by the Medical Congress, and examine these results, in order that the ground of its opinion may become apparent.

There was presented to this Congress, by a distinguished physician of New Jersey, Dr. Ezra M. Hunt, a paper on "Alcohol as a Food and Medicine," in which the whole subject is examined in the light of the most recent and carefully-conducted experiments of English, French, German and American chemists and physiologists, and their conclusions, as well as those of the author of the paper, set forth in the plainest manner. This has since been published by the National Temperance Society, and should be read and carefully studied by every one who is seeking for accurate information on the important subject we are now considering. It is impossible for us to more than glance at the evidence brought forward in proof of the assertion that and is exceedingly limited in its action as a remedial agent; and we, therefore, urge upon all who are interested in this subject, to possess themselves of Dr. Hunt's exhaustive treatise, and to study it carefully.

If the reader will refer to the quotation made by us in the second chapter from Dr. Henry Monroe, where the food value of any article is treated of, he will see it stated that "every kind of substance employed by man as food consists of sugar, starch, oil and glutinous matter, mingled together in various proportions; these are designed for the support of the animal frame. The glutinous principles of food—fibrine, albumen and casein—are employed to build up the structure; while the oil, starch and sugar are chiefly used to generate heat in the body."

Now, it is clear, that if alcohol is a food, it will be found to contain one or more of these substances. There must be in it either the nitrogenous elements found chiefly in meats, eggs, milk, vegetables and seeds, out of which animal tissue is built and waste repaired; or the carbonaceous elements found in fat, starch and sugar, in the consumption of which heat and force are evolved.

"The distinctness of these groups of foods," says Dr. Hunt, "and their relations to the tissue-producing and heat-evolving capacities of man, are so definite and so confirmed by experiments on animals and by manifold tests of scientific, physiological and clinical experience, that no attempt to discard the classification has prevailed. To draw so straight a line of demarcation as to limit the one entirely to tissue or cell production, and the other to heat and force production through ordinary combustion, and to deny any power of interchangeability under special demands or amid defective supply of one variety, is, indeed, untenable. This does not in the least invalidate the fact that we are able to use these as ascertained landmarks."

How these substances, when taken into the body, are assimilated, and how they generate force, are well known to the chemist and physiologist, who is able, in the light of well-ascertained laws, to determine whether alcohol does or does not possess a food value. For years, the ablest men in tne medical profession have given this subject the most careful study, and have subjected alcohol to every known test and experiment, and the result is that it has been, by common consent, excluded from the class of tissue-building foods. "We have never," says Dr. Hunt, "seen but a single suggestion that it could so act, and this a promiscuous guess. One writer (Hammond) thinks it possible that it may 'somehow' enter into combination with the products of decay in tissues, and 'under certain circumstances might yield *their* nitrogen to the construction of new tissues.' No parallel in organic chemistry, nor any evidence in animal chemistry, can be found to surround this guess with the areola of a possible hypothesis."

Dr. Richardson says: "Alcohol contains no nitrogen; it has none of the qualities of structure-building foods; it is incapable of being transformed into any of them; it is, therefore, not a food in any sense of its being a constructive agent in building up the body." Dr. W. B. Carpenter says: "Alcohol cannot supply anything which is essential to the true nutrition of the tissues." Dr. Liebig says: "Beer, wine, spirits, etc., furnish no element capable of entering into the composition of the blood, muscular fibre, or any part which is the seat of the principle of life." Dr. Hammond, in his Tribune Lectures, in which he advocates the use of alcohol in certain cases, says: "It is not demonstrable that alcohol undergoes conversion into tissue." Cameron, in his Manuel of Hygiene, says: "There is nothing in alcohol with which any part of the body can be nourished." Dr. E. Smith, F. R. S., says: "Alcohol is not a true food. It interferes with alimentation." Dr. T. K. Chambers says: "It is clear that we must cease to regard alcohol, as in any sense, a food."

"Not detecting in this substance," says Dr. Hunt, "any tissue-making ingredients, nor in its breaking up any combinations, such as we are able to trace in the cell foods, nor any evidence either in the experience of physiologists or the trials of alimentarians, it is not wonderful that in it we should find neither the expectancy nor the realization of constructive power."

Not finding in alcohol anything out of which the body can be built up or its waste supplied, it is next to be examined as to its heat-producing quality.

ALCOHOL NOT A PRODUCER OF HEAT.

"The first usual test for a force-producing food," says Dr. Hunt, "and that to which other foods of that class respond, is the production of heat in the combination of oxygen therewith. This heat means vital force, and is, in no small degree, a measure of the comparative value of the so-called respiratory foods. * * * If we examine the fats, the starches and the sugars, we can trace and estimate the processes by which they evolve heat and are changed into vital force, and can weigh the capacities of different foods. We find that the consumption of carbon by union with oxygen is the law, that heat is the product, and that the legitimate result is force, while the result of the union of the hydrogen of the foods with oxygen is water. If alcohol comes at all under this class of foods, we rightly expect to find some of the evidences which attach to the hydrocarbons."

What, then, is the result of experiments in this direction? They have been conducted through long periods and with the greatest care, by men of the highest attainments in chemistry and physiology, and the result is given in these few words, by Dr.

H. R. Wood, Jr., in his Materi Medica. "No one has been able to detect in the blood any of the ordinary results of its oxidation." That is, no one has been able to find that alcohol has undergone combustion, like fat, or starch, or sugar, and so given heat to the body. On the contrary, it is now known and admitted by the medical profession that

ALCOHOL REDUCES THE TEMPERATURE OF THE BODY,

instead of increasing it; and it has even been used in fevers as an anti-pyretic. So uniform has been the testimony of physicians in Europe and this country as to the cooling effects of alcohol, that Dr. Wood says, in his Materia Medica, "that it does not seem worth while to occupy space with a discussion of the subject." Liebermeister, one of the most learned contributors to Zeimssen's Cyclopædia of the Practice of Medicine, 1875, says: "I long since convinced myself, by direct experiments, that alcohol, even in comparatively large doses, does not elevate the temperature of the body in either well or sick people." So well had this become known to Arctic voyagers, that, even before physiologists had demonstrated the fact that alcohol reduced, instead of increasing, the temperature of the body, they had learned that spirits lessened their power to withstand extreme cold. "In the Northern regions," says Edward Smith, "it was proved that the entire exclusion of spirits was necessary, in order to retain heat under these unfavorable conditions."

ALCOHOL DOES NOT GIVE STRENGTH.

If alcohol does not contain tissue-building material, nor give heat to the body, it cannot possibly add to its strength. "Every kind of power an animal can generate," says Dr. G. Budd, F. R. S., "the mechanical power of the muscles, the chemical (or digestive) power of the stomach, the intellectual power of the brain—accumulates *through the nutrition of the organ* on which it depends.' Dr. F. R. Lees, of Edinburgh, after discussing the question, and educing evidence, remarks: "From the very nature of things, it will now be seen how *impossible* it is that alcohol can be strengthening food of either kind. Since it cannot become a *part* of the body, it cannot consequently contribute to its cohesive, organic strength, or fixed power; and, since it comes out of the body just as it went in, it cannot, by its decomposition, generate *heat*-force."

Sir Benjamin Brodie says: "Stimulants do not create nervous power; they merely enable you, as it were, to *use up* that which is left, and then they leave you more in need of rest than before."

Baron Liebig, so far back as 1843, in his "Animal Chemistry," pointed out the fallacy of alcohol generating power. He says: "The circulation will appear accelerated at the expense of the force available for voluntary motion, but without the production of a greater amount of mechanical force." In his later "Letters," he again says: "Wine is quite superfluous to man, * * * it is constantly followed by the expenditure of power"—whereas, the real function of food is to give power. He adds: "These drinks promote the change of matter in the body, and are, consequently, attended by an inward loss of power, which ceases to be productive, because it is not employed in overcoming outward difficulties—*i. e.*, in working." In other words, this great chemist asserts that alcohol abstracts the power of the system from doing useful work in the field or workshop, in order to cleanse the house from the defilement of alcohol itself.

The late Dr. W. Brinton, Physician to St. Thomas', in his great work on Dietetics, says: "Careful observation leaves little doubt that a moderate dose of beer or wine would, in most cases, at once diminish the maximum weight which a healthy person could lift. Mental acuteness, accuracy of perception and delicacy of the senses are all so far opposed by alcohol, as that the maximum efforts of each are incompatible with the ingestion of any moderate quantity of fermented liquid. A single glass will often suffice to take the edge off both mind and body, and to reduce their capacity to something below their perfection of work."

Dr. F. R. Lees, F. S. A., writing on the subject of alcohol as a food, makes the following quotation from an essay on "Stimulating Drinks," published by Dr. H. R. Madden, as long ago as 1847: "Alcohol is not the natural stimulus to any of our organs, and hence, functions performed in consequence of its application, tend to debilitate the organ acted upon.

"Alcohol is incapable of being assimilated or converted into any organic proximate principle, and hence, cannot be considered nutritious.

"The strength experienced after the use of alcohol is not new strength added to the system, but is manifested by calling into exercise the nervous energy pre-existing.

"The ultimate exhausting effects of alcohol, owing to its stimulant properties, produce an unnatural susceptibility to morbid action in all the organs, and this, with the plethora superinduced, becomes a fertile source of disease.

"A person who habitually exerts himself to such an extent as to require the daily use of stimulants to ward off exhaustion, may be compared to a machine working under high pressure. He will become much more obnoxious to the causes of disease, and will certainly break down sooner than he would have done under more favorable circumstances.

"The more frequently alcohol is had recourse to for the purpose of overcoming feelings of debility, the more it will be required, and by constant repetition a period is at length reached when it cannot be foregone, unless reaction is simultaneously brought about by a temporary total change of the habits of life.

"Owing to the above facts, I conclude that the DAILY USE OF STIMULANTS IS INDEFENSIBLE UNDER ANY KNOWN CIRCUMSTANCES."

DRIVEN TO THE WALL.

Not finding that alcohol possesses any direct alimentary value, the medical advocates of its use have been driven to the assumption that it is a kind of secondary food, in that it has the power to delay the metamorphosis of tissue "By the metamorphosis of tissue is meant," says Dr. Hunt, "that change which is constantly going on in the system which involves a constant disintegration of material; a breaking up and avoiding of that which is no longer aliment, making room for that new supply which is to sustain life." Another medical writer, in referring to this metamorphosis, says: "The importance of this process to the maintenance of life is readily shown by the injurious effects which follow upon its disturbance. If the discharge of the excrementitious substances be in any way impeded or suspended, these substances accumulate either in the blood or tissues, or both. In consequence of this retention and accumulation they become poisonous, and rapidly produce a derangement of the vital functions. Their influence is principally exerted upon the nervous system, through which they produce most frequent irritability, disturbance of the special senses, delirium, insensibility, coma, and finally, death."

"This description," remarks Dr. Hunt, "seems almost intended for alcohol." He then says: "To claim alcohol as a food because it delays the metamorphosis of tissue, is to claim that it in some way suspends the normal conduct of the laws of assimilation and nutrition, of waste and repair. A leading advocate of alcohol (Hammond) thus illustrates it: 'Alcohol retards the destruction of the tissues. By this destruction, force is generated, muscles contract, thoughts are developed, organs secrete and excrete.' In other words, alcohol interferes with all these. No wonder the author 'is not clear' how it does this, and we are not clear how such delayed metamorphosis recuperates. To take an agent which is

NOT KNOWN TO BE IN ANY SENSE AN ORIGINATOR OF VITAL FORCE;

which is not known to have any of the usual power of foods, and use it on the double assumption that it delays metamorphosis of tissue, and that such delay is conservative of health, is to pass outside of the bounds of science into the land of remote possibilities, and confer the title of adjuster upon an agent whose agency is itself doubtful. * * * *

"Having failed to identify alcohol as a nitrogenous or non-nitrogenous food, not having found it amenable to any of the evidences by which the food-force of aliments is generally measured, it will not do for us to talk of benefit by delay of regressive metamorphosis unless such process is accompanied with something evidential of the fact—something scientifically descriptive of its mode of accomplishment in the case at hand, and unless it is shown to be practically desirable for alimentation.

"There can be no doubt that alcohol does cause

defects in the processes of elimination which are natural to the healthy body and which even in disease are often conservative of health. In the pent-in evils which pathology so often shows occurrent in the case of spirit-drinkers, in the vascular, fatty and fibroid degenerations which take place, in the accumulations of rheumatic and scrofulous tendencies, there is the strongest evidence that

ALCOHOL ACTS AS A DISTURBING ELEMENT

and is very prone to initiate serious disturbances amid the normal conduct both of organ and function.

"To assert that this interference is conservative in the midst of such a fearful accumulation of evidence as to result in quite the other direction, and that this kind of delay in tissue-change accumulates vital force, is as unscientific as it is paradoxical.

"Dickinson, in his able expose of the effects of alcohol, (*Lancet*, Nov., 1872,) confines himself to pathological facts. After recounting, with accuracy, the structural changes which it initiates, and the structural changes and consequent derangement and suspension of vital functions which it involves, he aptly terms it the 'genius of degeneration.'

"With abundant provision of indisputable foods, select that liquid which has failed to command the general assent of experts that it is a food at all, and because it is claimed to diminish some of the excretions, call that a delay of metamorphosis of tissue conservative of health! The ostrich may bury his head in the sand, but science will not close its eyes before such impalpable dust."

Speaking of this desperate effort to claim alcohol as a food, Dr. N. S. Davis well says: "It seems hardly possible that men of eminent attainments in the profession should so far forget one of the most fundamental and universally recognized laws of organic life as to promulgate the fallacy here stated. The fundamental law to which we allude is, that all vital phenomena are accompanied by, and dependent on, molecular or atomic changes; and whatever retards these retards the phenomena of life; whatever suspends these suspends life. Hence, to say that an agent which retards tissue metamorphosis is in any sense a food, is simply to pervert and misapply terms."

Well may the author of the paper from which we have quoted so freely, exclaim: "Strangest ot foods! most impalpable of aliments! defying all the research of animal chemistry, tasking all the ingenuity of experts in hypothetical explanations, registering its effects chiefly by functional disturbance and organic lesions, causing its very defenders as a food to stultify themselves when in fealty to facts they are compelled to disclose its destructions, and to find the only defense in that line of demarcation, more imaginary than the equator, more delusive than the mirage, between use and abuse."

That alcohol is not a food in any sense, has been fully shown; and now,

WHAT IS ITS VALUE AS A MEDICINE?

Our reply to this question will be brief. The reader has, already, the declaration of the International Medical Congress, that, as a medicine, the range of alcohol is limited and doubtful, and that its self-prescription by the laity should be utterly discountenanced by the profession. No physician who has made himself thoroughly acquainted with the effects of alcohol when introduced into the blood and brought in contact with the membranes, nerves and organs of the human body, would now venture to prescribe its free use to consumptives as was done a very few years ago.

"In the whole management of lung diseases," remarks Dr. Hunt, "with the exception of the few who can always be relied upon to befriend alcohol, other remedies have largely superseded all spirituous liquors. Its employment in stomach disease, once so popular, gets no encouragement, from a careful examination of its local and constitutional effects, as separated from the water, sugar and acids imbibed with it."

TYPHOID FEVER.

It is in typhoid fever that alcohol has been used, perhaps, most frequently by the profession; but this use is now restricted, and the administration made with great caution. Prof. A. L. Loomis, of New

York City, has published several lectures on the pathology and treatment of typhoid fever. Referring thereto, Dr. Hunt says: "No one in our country can speak more authoritatively, and as he has no radical views as to the exclusion of alcohol, it is worth while to notice the place to which he assigns it. In the milder cases he entirely excludes it. As a means of reducing temperature, he does not mention it, but relies on cold, quinine, and sometimes, digitalis and quinine." When, about the third week, signs of failure of heart-power begin to manifest themselves, and the use of some form of stimulant seems to be indicated, Dr. Loomis gives the most guarded advice as to their employment. "Never," he says, "give a patient stimulants simply because he has typhoid fever." And again, "Where there is reasonable doubt as to the propriety of giving or withholding stimulants, it is safer to withhold them." He then insists that, if stimulants are administered, the patient should be visited every two hours to watch their effects.

It will thus be seen how guarded has now become the use of alcohol as a cardiac stimulant in typhoid fevers, where it was once employed with an almost reckless freedom. Many practitioners have come to exclude it altogether, and to rely wholly on ammonia, ether and foods.

In Cameron's "Hygiene" is this sentence: "In candor, it must be admitted that many eminent physicians deny the efficacy of alcohol in the treatment of any kind of disease, *and some assert that it is worse than useless.*"

ACCUMULATIVE TESTIMONY.

Dr. Arnold Lees, F. L. S., in a recent paper on the "Use and Action of Alcohol in Disease," assumes "*that the old use of alcohol was not science, but a grave blunder.*" Prof. C. A. Parks says: "It is impossible not to feel that, so far, the progress of physiological inquiry renders the use of alcohol (in medicine) more and more doubtful." Dr. Anstie says: "If alcohol is to be administered at all for the *relief* of neuralgia, it should be given with as much precision, as to dose, as we should use in giving an acknowledged *deadly poison.*" Dr. F. T. Roberts, an eminent English physician, in advocating a guarded use of alcohol in typhoid fever, says: "Alcoholic stimulants are, by no means, always required, and their indiscriminate use may do a great deal of harm." In Asiatic cholera, brandy was formerly administered freely to patients when in the stage of collapse. The effect was injurious, instead of beneficial. "Again and again," says Prof. G. Johnson, "have I seen a patient grow colder, and his pulse diminish in volume and power, after a dose of brandy, and, apparently, as a direct result of the brandy." And Dr. Pidduck, of London, who used common salt in cholera treatment, says: "Of eighty-six cases in the stage of collapse, sixteen only proved fatal, and scarcely one would have died, *if I had been able to prevent them from taking brandy and laudanum.*" Dr. Collenette, of Guernsey, says: "For more than thirty years I have abandoned the use of all kinds of alcoholic drinks in my practice, and with such good results, that, were I sick, *nothing* would induce *me* to have resource to them—*they are but noxious depressants.*"

As a non-professional writer, we cannot go beyond the medical testimony which has been educed, and we now leave it with the reader. We could add many pages to this testimony, but such cumulative evidence would add but little to its force with the reader. If he is not yet convinced that alcohol has no food value, and that, as a medicine, its range is exceedingly limited, and always of doubtful administration, nothing further that we might be able to cite or say could have any influence with him.

CHAPTER VI.

THE GROWTH AND POWER OF APPETITE.

ONE fact attendant on habitual drinking stands out so prominently that none can call it in question. It is that of the steady growth of appetite. There are exceptions, as in the action of nearly every rule; but the almost invariable result of the habit we have mentioned, is, as we have said, a steady growth of appetite for the stimulant imbibed. That this is in consequence of certain morbid changes in the physical condition produced by the alcohol itself, will hardly be questioned by any one who has made himself acquainted with the various functional and organic derangements which invariably follow the continued introduction of this substance into the body.

But it is to the fact itself, not to its cause, that we now wish to direct the reader's attention. The man who is satisfied at first with a single glass of wine at dinner, finds, after awhile, that appetite asks for a little more; and, in time, a second glass is conceded. The increase of desire may be very slow, but it goes on surely until, in the end, a whole bottle will scarcely suffice, with far too many, to meet its imperious demands. It is the same in regard to the use of every other form of alcoholic drink.

Now, there are men so constituted that they are able, for a long series of years, or even for a whole lifetime, to hold this appetite within a certain limit of indulgence. To say "So far, and no farther." They suffer ultimately from physical ailments, which surely follow the prolonged contact of alcoholic poison with the delicate structures of the body, many of a painful character, and shorten the term of their natural lives; but still they are able to drink without an increase of appetite so great as to reach an overmastering degree. They do not become abandoned drunkards.

NO MAN SAFE WHO DRINKS.

But no man who begins the use of alcohol in any form can tell what, in the end, is going to be its effect on his body or mind. Thousands and tens of thousands, once wholly unconscious of danger from this source, go down yearly into drunkards' graves. There is no standard by which any one can measure the latent evil forces in his inherited nature. He may have from ancestors, near or remote, an unhealthy moral tendency, or physical diathesis, to which the peculiarly disturbing influence of alcohol will give the morbid condition in which it will find its disastrous life. That such results follow the use of alcohol in a large number of cases, is now a well-known fact in the history of inebriation. During the past few years, the subject of alcoholism, with the mental and moral causes leading thereto, have attracted a great deal of earnest attention. Physicians, superintendents of inebriate and lunatic asylums, prison-keepers, legislators and philanthropists have been observing and studying its many sad and terrible phases, and recording results and opinions. While differences are held on some points, as, for instance, whether drunkenness is a disease for which, after it has been established, the individual ceases to be responsible, and should be subject to restraint and treatment, as for lunacy or fever; a crime to be punished; or a sin to be repented of and healed by the Physician of souls, all agree that there is an inherited or acquired mental and nervous condition with many, which renders any use of alcohol exceedingly dangerous.

The point we wish to make with the reader is, that no man can possibly know, until he has used alcoholic drinks for a certain period of time, whether he has or has not this hereditary or acquired physical or mental condition; and that, if it should exist, a discovery of the fact may come too late.

Dr. D. G. Dodge, late Superintendent of the New York State Inebriate Asylum, speaking of the causes leading to intemperance, after stating his belief that it is a transmissible disease, like "scrofula, gout or consumption," says:

"There are men who have an organization, which may be termed an alcoholic idiosyncrasy; with them the latent desire for stimulants, if indulged, soon leads to habits of intemperance, and eventually to a morbid appetite, which has all the characteristics of a diseased condition of the system, which the patient, unassisted, is powerless to relieve—since the weakness of the will that led to the disease obstructs its removal.

"Again, we find in another class of persons, those who have had healthy parents, and have been educated and accustomed to good social influences, moral and social, but whose temperament and physical constitution are such, that, when they once indulge in the use of stimulants, which they find pleasurable, they continue to habitually indulge till they cease to be moderate, and become excessive drinkers. A depraved appetite is established, that leads them on slowly, but surely, to destruction."

A DANGEROUS DELUSION.

In this chapter, our chief purpose is to show the growth and awful power of an appetite which begins striving for the mastery the moment it is indulged, and against the encroachments of which no man who gives it any indulgence is absolutely safe. He who so regards himself is resting in a most dangerous delusion. So gradually does it increase, that few observe its steady accessions of strength until it has acquired the power of a master. Dr. George M. Burr, in a paper on the pathology of drunkenness, read before the "American Association for the Cure of Inebriates," says, in referring to the first indications of an appetite, which he considers one of the symptoms of a forming disease, says: "This early stage is marked by an occasional desire to drink, which recurs at shorter and shorter intervals, and a propensity, likewise, gradually increasing for a greater quantity at each time. This stage has long been believed to be one of voluntary indulgence, for which the subject of it was morally responsible. The drinker has been held as criminal for his occasional indulgence, and his example has been most severely censured. This habit, however, must be regarded as the first intimation of the approaching disease—the stage of invasion, precisely as sensations of *mal-aise* and chills usher in a febrile attack.

"It is by no means claimed that in this stage the subject is free from responsibility as regards the consequences of his acts, or that his case is to be looked upon as beyond all attempts at reclamation. Quite to the contrary. This is the stage for active interference. Restraint, prohibition, quarantine, anything may be resorted to, to arrest the farther advance of the disease. Instead of being taught that the habit of occasional drinking is merely a moral *lapsus* (not the most powerful restraining motive always), the subject of it should be made to understand that it is the commencement of a malady, which, if unchecked, will overwhelm him in ruin, and, compared with which, cholera and yellow fever are harmless. He should be impressed with the fact that the early stage is the one when recuperation is most easy—that the will then has not lost its power of control, and that the fatal propensity is not incurable. The duty of prevention, or avoidance, should be enforced with as much earnestness and vigor as we are required to carry out sanitary measures against the spread of small-pox or any infectious disease. The subject of inebriety may be justly held responsible, if he neglects all such efforts, and allows the disease to progress without a struggle to arrest it.

"The formative stage of inebriety continues for a longer or shorter period, when, as is well known, more frequent repetitions of the practice of drinking are to be observed. The impulse to drink grows stronger and stronger, the will-power is overthrown and the entire organism becomes subject to the fearful demands for stimulus. It is now that the stage of confirmed inebriation is formed, and *dypso-mania* fully established. The constant introduction of alcohol into the system, circulating with the fluids and permeating the tissues, adds fuel to the already enkindled flame, and intensifies the propensity to an irresistible degree. Nothing now satisfies short of complete intoxication, and, until the unhappy subject of the disease falls senseless and completely overcome, will he cease his efforts to gratify this most insatiable desire."

Dr. Alexander Peddie, of Edinburgh, who has given twenty years of study to this subject, remarked, in his testimony before a Committee of the House of Commons, that there seemed to be "a peculiar elective affinity for the action of alcohol on the nervous system after it had found its way through the circulation into the brain," by which the whole organism was disturbed, and the man rendered less able to resist morbid influences of any kind. He gave many striking instances of the growth and power of appetite, which had come under his professional notice, and of the ingenious devices and desperate resorts to which dypsomaniacs were driven in their efforts to satisfy their inordinate cravings. No consideration, temporal or spiritual, had any power to restrain their appetite, if, by any means, fair or foul, they could obtain alcoholic stimulants. To get this, he said, the unhappy subject of this terrible thirst "will tell the most shameful lies—for no truth is ever found in connection with the habitual drunkard's state. He never yet saw truth in relation to drink got out of one who was a dysomaniac—he has sufficient reason left to tell these untruths, and to understand his position, because people in that condition are seldom dead drunk; they are seldom in the condition of total stupidity; they have generally an eye open to their own affairs, and that which is the main business of their existence, namely, how to get drink. They will resort to the most ingenious, mean and degrading contrivances and practices to procure and conceal liquor, and this, too, while closely watched; and will succeed in deception, although fabulous quantities are daily swallowed."

Dr. John Nugent gives a case which came within his own knowledge, of a lady who had been

A MOST EXEMPLARY NUN

for fifteen or twenty years. In consequence of her devotion to the poor, attending them in fevers, and like cases, it seemed necessary for her to take stimulants; these stimulants grew to be habitual, and she had been compelled, five or six times, to place herself in a private asylum. In three or four weeks after being let out, she would relapse, although she was believed to be under the strongest influences of religion, and of the most virtuous desires. There had been developed in her that disposition to drink which she was unable to overcome or control.

The power of this appetite, and the frightful moral perversions that often follow its indulgence are vividly portrayed in the following extract, from an address by Dr. Elisha Harris, of New York, in which he discusses the question of the criminality of drunkenness.

"Let the fact be noticed that such is the lethargy which alcoholism produces upon reason and conscience, that it is sometimes necessary to bring the offender to view his drunken indulgence as a crime. We have known a refined and influential citizen to be so startled at the fact that he wished to destroy the lives of all persons, even of his own family, who manifested unhappiness at his intemperance, that seeing this terrible criminality of his indulgence, instantly formed, and has forever kept, his resolutions of abstinence. We have known the hereditary dypsomaniac break from his destroyer, and when tempted in secret by the monstrous appetite, so grind his teeth and clinch his jaws in keeping his vows to taste not, that blood dripped from his mouth and cold sweat bathed his face. That man is a model of temperance and moral power to-day. And it was the consciousness of personal criminality that stimulated these successful conflicts with the morbid appetite and the powers of the alcohol disease that had fastened upon them. Shall we hesitate to hold ourselves, or to demand that communities shall hold every drunkard—not yet insane—responsible for every act of inebriety? Certainly, it is not cruel or unjust to deal thus with drunkenness. It is not the prison we open, but conscience."

The danger in which those stand who have an

INHERITED PREDISPOSITION TO DRINK,

is very great. Rev. I. Willett, Superintendent of the Inebriate's Home, Fort Hamilton, Kings County, New York, thus refers to this class, which is larger than many think: "There are a host of living men and women to be found who never drank, and who dare not drink, intoxicating liquors or beverages, because one or both of their parents were inebriates before they were born into the world; and, besides, a number of these have brothers or sisters who, having given way to the inherited appetite, are now passing downward on this descending sliding scale. The greater portion of them have already passed over the bounds of self-control, and the varied preliminary symptoms of melancholy, mania, paralysis, ideas of persecution, etc., etc., are developing. As to the question of responsibility, each case is either more or less doubtful, and can only be tested on its separate merits. There is, however, abundant evidence to prove that this predisposition to inebriety, even after long indulgence, can, by a skillful process of medication, accompanied by either voluntary or compulsory restraint, be subdued; and the counterbalancing physical and mental powers can at the same time be so strengthened and invigorated as in the future to enable the person to resist the temptations by which he may be surrounded. Yea, though the powers of reason may, for the time being, be dethroned, and lunacy be developed, these cases, in most instances, will yield to medical treatment where the surrounding conditions of restraint and careful nursing are supplemental.

"We have observed that in many instances the fact of the patient being convinced that he is an hereditary inebriate, has produced beneficial results. Summoning to his aid all the latent counterbalancing energies which he has at command, and clothing himself with this armor, he goes forth to war, throws up the fortifications of physical and mental restraint, repairs the breaches and inroads of diseased appetite, regains control of the citadel of the brain, and then, with shouts of triumph, he unfurls the banner of 'VICTORY!'"

Dr. Wood, of London, in his work on insanity, speaking on the subject of hereditary inebriety, says:

"Instances are sufficiently familiar, and several have occurred within my own personal knowledge, where the father, having died at any early age from the effects of intemperance, has left a son to be brought up by those who have severely suffered from his excesses, and have therefore the strongest motives to prevent, if possible, a repetition of such misery; every pains has been taken to enforce sobriety, and yet, notwithstanding all precautions, the habits of the father have become those of the son, who, never having seen him from infancy, could not have adopted them from imitation. Everything was done to encourage habits of temperance, but all to no purpose; the seeds of the disease had begun to germinate; a blind impulse led the doomed individual, by successive and rapid strides, along the same course which was fatal to the father, and which, ere long, terminated in his own destruction."

How great and fearful the power of an appetite which cannot only enslave and curse the man over which it gains control, but send its malign influence down to the second and third and fourth generations, sometimes to the absolute

EXTINGUISHMENT OF FAMILIES!

Morel, a Frenchman, gives the following as the result of his observation of the hereditary effects of drunkenness:

"*First generation:* Immorality, depravity, excess in the use of alcoholic liquors, moral debasement. *Second generation:* Hereditary drunkenness, paroxysms of mania, general paralysis. *Third generation:* Sobriety, hypochondria, melancholy, systematic ideas of being persecuted, homicidal tendencies. *Fourth generation:* Intelligence slightly developed, first accessions of mania at sixteen years of age, stupidity, subsequent idiocy and probable extinction of family."

Dr. T. D. Crothers, in an analysis of the hundred cases of inebriety received at the New York Inebriate Asylum, gives this result: "Inebriety inherited direct from parents was traced in twenty-one cases. In eleven of these the father drank alone, in six instances the mother drank, and in four cases both parents drank.

"In thirty-three cases inebriety was traced to ancestors more remote, as grandfather, grandmother, etc., etc., the collateral branches exhibiting both inebriety and insanity. In some instances a whole generation had been passed over, and the disorders of the grandparents appeared again.

"In twenty cases various neurosal disorders had been prominent in the family and its branches, of which neuralgia, chorea, hysteria, eccentricity, mania, epilepsy and inebriety, were most common.

"In some cases, a wonderful periodicity in the outbreak of these disorders was manifested.

"For instance, in one family, for two generations, inebriety appeared in seven out of twelve members, after they had passed forty, and ended fatally within ten years. In another, hysteria, chorea, epilepsy and mania, with drunkenness, came on soon after puberty, and seemed to deflect to other disorders, or exhaust itself before middle life. This occurred in eight out of fourteen, extending over two generations. In another instance, the descendants of three generations, and many of the collateral branches, developed inebriety, mental eccentricities, with other disorders bordering on mania, at about thirty-five years of age. In some cases this lasted only a few years, in others a lifetime."

And here let us say that in this matter of an inherited appetite there is a difference of views with some who believe that appetite is never transmitted but always acquired. This difference of view is more apparent than real. It is not the drunkard's appetite that is transmitted, but the bias or proclivity which renders the subject of such an inherited tendency more susceptible to exciting causes, and therefore in greater danger from the use of alcoholic drinks than others.

Dr. N. S. Davis, in an article in the *Washingtonian*, published at Chicago, presents the opposite view of the case. The following extract from this article is well worthy to be read and considered:

"If we should say that man is so constituted that he is capable of feeling weary, restless, despondent and anxious, and that he instinctively desires to be relieved of these unpleasant feelings, we should assert a self-evident fact. And we should thereby assert all the instincts or natural impulse there is in the matter. It is simply a desire to be relieved from unpleasant feelings, and does not, in the slightest degree, indicate or suggest any particular remedy. It no more actually suggests the idea of alcohol or opium than it does bread and water. But if, by accident, or by the experience of others, the individual has learned that his unpleasant feelings can be relieved, for the time being, by alcohol, opium or any other exhilarant, he not only uses the remedy himself, but perpetuates a knowledge of the same to others. It is in this way, and this only, that most of the nations and tribes of our race, have, much to their detriment, found a knowledge of some kind of intoxicant. The same explanation is applicable to the supposed 'constitutional susceptibility,' as a primary cause of intemperance. That some persons inherit a greater degree of nervous and organic susceptibility than others, and are, in consequence of this greater susceptibility, more readily affected by a given quantity of narcotic, anæsthetic or intoxicant, is undoubtedly true. And that such will

MORE READILY BECOME DRUNKARDS,

if they once commence to use intoxicating drinks, is also true. But that such persons, or any others, have the slightest inherent or constitutional taste or any longing for intoxicants, until they have acquired such taste or longing by actual use, we find no reliable proof. It is true that statistics appear to show that a larger proportion of the children of drunkards become themselves drunkards, than of children born of total abstainers. And hence the conclusion has been drawn that such children INHERITED the constitutional tendency to inebriation. But before we are justified in adopting such a conclusion, several other important facts must be ascertained.

"1st. We must know whether the mother, while nursing, used more or less constantly some kind of alcoholic beverage, by which the alcohol might have impregnated the milk in her breasts and thereby made its early impression on the tastes and longings of the child.

"2d. We must know whether the intemperate parents were in the habit of frequently giving alcoholic preparations to the children, either to relieve temporary ailments, or for the same reason that they drank it themselves. I am constrained to say, that from my own observation, extending over a period of forty years, and a field by no means limited, I am satisfied that nineteen out of every twenty persons who have been regarded as HEREDITARY inebriates have simply ACQUIRED the disposition to drink by one or both of the methods just mentioned, after birth."

The views here presented in no way lessen but really heighten the perils of moderate drinking. It is affirmed that some persons inherit a greater degree of nervous and organic susceptibility than others, and are, in consequence, more readily affected by a given quantity of narcotic, anæsthetic or intoxicant; *and that such "will more readily become drunkards if they commence to use intoxicating drinks."*

Be the cause of this

INHERITED NERVOUS SUSCEPTIBILITY

what it may, and it is far more general than is to be inferred from the admission just quoted, the fact stands forth as a solemn warning of the peril every man encounters in even the most moderate use of alcohol. Speaking of this matter, Dr. George M. Beard, who is not as sound on the liquor question as we could wish, says, in an article on the "Causes of the Recent Increase of Inebriety in America:" "As a means of prevention, abstinence from the *habit* of drinking is to be enforced. Such abstinence may not have been necessary for our fathers, but it is rendered necessary for a large body of the American people on account of our greater nervous susceptibility. It is possible to drink without being an habitual drinker, as it is possible to take chloral or opium without forming the habit of taking these substances. In certain countries and climates where the nervous system is strong and the temperature more equable than with us, in what I sometimes call the temperate belt of the world, including Spain, Italy, Southern France, Syria and Persia, the habitual use of wine rarely leads to drunkenness, and never, or almost never, to inebriety; but in the intemperate belt, where we live, and which includes Northern Europe and the United States, with a cold and violently changeable climate, the habit of drinking either wines or stronger liquors is liable to develop in some cases a habit of intemperance. Notably in our country, where nervous sensitiveness is seen in its extreme manifestations, the majority of brain-workers are not safe so long as they are in the habit of even moderate drinking. I admit that this was not the case one hundred years ago—and the reasons I have already given—it is not the case to-day in Continental Europe; even in England it is not so markedly the case as in the northern part of the United States. *For those individuals who inherit a tendency to inebriety, the only safe course is absolute abstinence, especially in early life.*"

In the same article, Dr. Baird remarks: "The number of those in this country who cannot bear tea, coffee or alcoholic liquors of any kind, is very large. There are many, especially in the Northern

States, who must forego coffee entirely, and use tea only with caution; either, in any excess, cause trembling nerves and sleepless nights. The susceptibility to alcohol is so marked, with many persons, that no pledges, and no medical advice, and no moral or legal influences are needed to keep them in the paths of temperance. *Such persons are warned by flushing of the face, or by headache, that alcohol, whatever it may be to others, or whatever it may have been to their ancestors, is poison to them.*"

But, in order to give a higher emphasis to precepts, admonition and medical testimony, we offer a single example of the enslaving power of appetite, when, to a predisposing hereditary tendency, the excitement of indulgence has been added. The facts of this case were communicated to us by a professional gentleman connected with one of our largest inebriate asylums, and we give them almost in his very words in which they were related.

A REMARKABLE CASE.

A clever, but dissipated actor married clandestinely a farmer's daughter in the State of New York. The parents of the girl would not recognize him as the husband of their child; rejecting him so utterly that he finally left the neighborhood. A son born of this marriage gave early evidence of great mental activity, and was regarded, in the college where he graduated, as almost a prodigy of learning. He carried off many prizes, and distinguished himself as a brilliant orator. Afterwards he went to Princeton and studied for the ministry. While there, it was discovered that he was secretly drinking. The faculty did everything in their power to help and restrain him; and his co-operation with them was earnest as to purpose, but not permanently availing. The nervous susceptibility inherited from his father responded with a morbid quickness to every exciting cause, and the moment wine or spirits touched the sense of smell or taste, he was seized with an almost irresistible desire to drink to excess, and too often yielded to its demands. For months he would abstain entirely; and then drink to intoxication in secret.

After graduating from Princeton he became pastor of a church in one of the largest cities of Western New York, where he remained for two years, distinguishing himself for his earnest work and fervid eloquence. But the appetite he had formed was imperious in its demands, and periodically became so strong that he lost the power of resistance. When these periodic assaults of appetite came, he would

LOCK HIMSELF IN HIS ROOM FOR DAYS

and satiate the fierce thirst, coming out sick and exhausted. It was impossible to conceal from his congregation the dreadful habit into which he had fallen, and ere two years had elapsed he was dismissed for drunkenness. He then went to one of the chief cities of the West, where he received a call, and was, for a time, distinguished as a preacher; but again he fell into disgrace and had to leave his charge. Two other churches called him to fill the office of pastor, but the same sad defections from sobriety followed. For a considerable time after this his friends lost sight of him. Then he was found in the streets of New York City by the president of the college from which he had first graduated, wretched and debased from drink, coatless and hatless. His old friend took him to a hotel, and then brought his case to the notice of the people at a prayer-meeting held in the evening at one of the churches. His case was immediately taken in hand and money raised to send him to the State Inebriate Asylum. After he had remained there for a year, he began to preach as a supply in a church a few miles distant, going on Saturday evening and returning on Monday morning; but always having an attendant with him, not daring to trust himself alone. This went on for nearly a whole year, when a revival sprang up in the church, which he conducted with great eloquence and fervor. After the second week of this new excitement, he began to lock himself up in his room after returning from the service, and could not be seen until the next morning. In the third week of the revival, the excitement of the meetings grew intense. After this he was only seen in the pulpit, where his air and manner were wild and thrilling. His friends at the asylum knew that he must be drinking, and while hesitating as to their wisest course, waited anxiously for the result. One day he was grandly eloquent. Such power in the pulpit had never been witnessed there before—his appeals were unequalled; but so wild and impassioned that some began to fear for his reason. At the close of this day's services, the chaplain of the institution of which he was an inmate, returned with him to the asylum, and on the way, told him frankly that he was deceiving the people—that his eloquent appeals came not from the power of he Holy Spirit, but from the excitement of drink; and that all farther conduct of the meetings must be left in other hands. On reaching the asylum he retired, greatly agitated, and soon after died from a stroke of apoplexy. In his room many empty bottles, which had contained brandy, were found; but the people outside remained in ignorance of the true cause of the marvelous eloquence which had so charmed and moved them.

We have already extended this chapter beyond the limit at first proposed. Our object has not only been to show the thoughtful and intelligent reader who uses alcoholic beverages, the great peril in which he stands, but to make apparent to every one, how insidious is the growth and how terrible the power of this appetite for intoxicants; an appetite which, if once established, is almost sure to rob its victim of honor, pity, tenderness and love; an appetite, whose indulgence too often transforms the man into a selfish demon. Think of it, all ye who dally with the treacherous cup; are not the risks you are running too great? Nay, considering your duties and your obligations, have you any right to run these risks?

And now that we have shown the curse of strong drink, let us see what agencies are at work in the abatement, prevention and cure of a disease that is undermining the health of whole nations, shortening the natural term of human life, and in our own country alone, sending over sixty thousand men and women annually into untimely graves.

Satan sends his trusted servants, Alcohol and Gambling, out upon a mission.

Alcohol meets a bright young man and cultivates his acquaintance.

Alcohol introduces the youth to his old-time friend, Gambling.

The mutual friends relieve the youth of his cash.

Alcohol and his victim have a jolly time.

The young man comes to grief, but Alcohol sticks by him.

They suggest an easy method for replenishing his exchequer.

The mutual friends determine to follow him to the inmost cell of the prison.

Alcohol and Gambling incite their victim to murder.

They mock him when upon the scaffold.

Alcohol and Gambling bury their victim in an untimely and dishonored grave.

They report their success to Satan and receive his congratulations.

CHAPTER VII.

MEANS OF CURE.

IS this disease, or vice, or sin, or crime of intemperance—call it by what name you will—increasing or diminishing? Has any impression been made upon it during the half-century in which there have been such earnest and untiring efforts to limit its encroachments on the health, prosperity, happiness and life of the people? What are the agencies of repression at work; how effective are they, and what is each doing?

These are questions full of momentous interest. Diseases of the body, if not cured, work a steady impairment of health, and bring pains and physical disabilities. If their assaults be upon nervous centres, or vital organs, the danger of paralysis or death becomes imminent. Now, as to this disease of intemperance, which is a social and moral as well as a physical disease, it is not to be concealed that it has invaded the common body of the people to an alarming degree, until, using the words of Holy Writ, "the whole head is sick and the whole heart faint." Nay, until, using a still stronger form of Scriptural illustration, "From the sole of the foot even unto the head, there is no soundness in it; but wounds and bruises and putrifying sores."

In this view, the inquiry as to increase or diminution, assumes the gravest importance. If, under all the agencies of cure and reform which have been in active operation during the past fifty years, no impression has been made upon this great evil which is so cursing the people, then is the case indeed desperate, if not hopeless. But if it appears that, under these varied agencies, there has been an arrest of the disease here, a limitation of its aggressive force there, its almost entire extirpation in certain cases, and a better public sentiment everywhere; then, indeed, may we take heart and say "God speed temperance work!" in all of its varied aspects.

HOPEFUL SIGNS.

And here, at the outset of our presentation of some of the leading agencies of reform and cure, let us say, that the evidence going to show that an impression has been made upon the disease is clear and indisputable; and that this impression is so marked as to give the strongest hope and assurance. In the face of prejudice, opposition, ridicule, persecution, obloquy and all manner of discouragements, the advocates of temperance have held steadily to their work these many years, and now the good results are seen on every hand. Contrast the public sentiment of to-day with that of twenty, thirty and forty years ago, and the progress becomes at once apparent. In few things is this so marked as in the changed attitude of the medical profession towards alcohol. One of the most dangerous, and, at the same time, one of the most securely intrenched of all our enemies, was the family doctor. Among his remedies and restoratives, wine, brandy, whisky and tonic ale all held a high place, and were administered more frequently, perhaps, than any other articles in the Materia Medica. The disease of his patients arrested by special remedies or broken by an effort of nature, he too often commenced the administration of alcohol in some one or more of its disguised and attractive forms, in order to give tone and stimulus to the stomach and nerves, and as a general vitalizer and restorative. The evil consequences growing out of this almost universal prescription of alcohol, were of the most lamentable character, and thousands and tens of thousands of men and women were betrayed into drunkenness. But to-day, you will not find a physician of any high repute in America or Europe who will give it to his patients, except in the most guarded manner and under the closest limitations; and he will not consent to any self-prescription whatever.

FRUITS OF TEMPERANCE WORK.

Is not this a great gain? And it has come as the result of temperance work and agitation, as Dr. Henry Monroe frankly admits in his lecture on the Physiological Action of Alcohol, where, after stating that his remarks would not partake of the character of a total abstinence lecture, but rather of a scientific inquiry into the mode of action of alcohol when introduced into the tissues of the body, he adds: "Nevertheless, I would not have it understood that I, in any way, disparage the moral efforts made by total abstainers who, years ago, amid good report and evil report, stood in the front of the battle to war against the multitude of evils occasioned by strong drink;—all praise be due to them for their noble and self-denying exertions! Had it not been for the successful labors of these moral giants in the great cause of temperance, presenting to the world in their own personal experiences many new and astounding physiological facts, *men of science would, probably, never have had their attention drawn to the topic.*"

Then, as a result of temperance work, we have a more restrictive legislation in many States, and prohibitory laws in New Hampshire, Vermont and Maine. In the State of Maine, a prohibitory law has been in operation for over twenty-six years; and so salutary has been the effect as seen in the

REDUCTION OF POVERTY, PAUPERISM AND CRIME,

that the Legislature, in January, 1877, added new and heavier penalties to the law, both Houses passing on the amendment without a dissenting voice. In all that State there is not, now, a single distillery or brewery in operation, nor a single open bar-room.

Forty years ago the pulpit was almost silent on the subject of intemperance and the liquor traffic; now, the church is fast arraying itself on the side of total abstinence and prohibition, and among its ministers are to be found many of our most active temperance workers.

Forty or fifty years ago, the etiquette of hospitality was violated if wine, or cordial, or brandy were not tendered. Nearly every sideboard had its display of decanters, well filled, and it was almost as much an offense for the guest to decline as for the host to omit the proffered glass. Even boys and girls were included in the custom; and tastes were acquired which led to drunkenness in after life. All this is changed now.

The curse of the liquor traffic is attracting, as never before, the attention of all civilized people; and national, State and local legislatures and governments are appointing commissions of inquiry, and gathering data and facts, with a view to its restriction.

And, more hopeful than all, signs are becoming more and more apparent that the people are everywhere awakening to a sense of the dangers that attend this traffic. Enlightenment is steadily progressing. Reason and judgment; common sense and prudence, are all coming to the aid of repression. Men see, as they never saw before, how utterly evil and destructive are the drinking habits of this and other nations; how they weaken the judgment and deprave the moral sense; how they not only take from every man who falls into them his ability to do his best in any pursuit or calling, but sow in his body the germs of diseases which will curse him in his later years and abridge their term.

Other evidences of the steady growth among the people of a sentiment adverse to drinking might be given. We see it in the almost feverish response that everywhere meets the strong appeals of temperance speakers, and in the more pronounced attitude taken by public and professional men.

JUDGES ON THE BENCH

and preachers from the pulpit alike lift their voices in condemnation. Grand juries repeat and repeat their presentations of liquor selling and liquor drinking as the fruitful source of more than two-thirds of the crimes and miseries that afflict the community; and prison reports add their painful emphasis to the warning of the inquest.

The people learn slowly, but they are learning. Until they *will* that this accursed traffic shall cease, it must go on with its sad and awful consequences. But the old will of the people has been debased by sensual indulgence. It is too weak to set itself against the appetite by which it has become enslaved. There must be a new will formed in the ground of enlightenment and intelligence; and then, out of knowing what is right and duty in regard to this great question of temperance and restriction, will come the will to do. And when we have this new will resting in the true enlightenment of the people, we shall have no impeded action. Whatever sets itself in opposition thereto must go down.

And for this the time is coming, though it may still be far off. Of its steady approach, the evidences are many and cheering. Meanwhile, we must work and wait. If we are not yet strong enough to drive out the enemy, we may limit his power, and do

THE WORK OF HEALING AND SAVING.

What, then, is being done in this work of healing and saving? Is there, in fact, any cure for the dreadful malady of drunkenness? Are men ever really saved from its curse? and, if so, how is it done, and what are the agencies employed?

Among the first of these to which we shall refer, is the pledge. As a means of reform and restriction, it has been used by temperance workers from the beginning, and still holds a prominent place. Seeing that only in a complete abstinence from intoxicating drinks was there any hope of rescue for the drunkard, or any security for the moderate drinker, it was felt that under a solemn pledge to wholly abstain from their use, large numbers of men would, from a sense of honor, self-respect or conscience, hold themselves free from touch or taste. In the case of moderate drinkers, with whom appetite is yet under control, the pledge has been of great value; but almost useless after appetite has gained the mastery.

In a simple pledge there is no element of self-control. If honor, self-respect or conscience, rallying to its support in the hour of temptation, be not stronger than appetite, it will be of no avail. And it too often happens that, with the poor inebriate, these have become blunted, or well-nigh extinguished. The consequence has been that where the pledge has been solely relied upon, the percentage of reform has been very small. As a first means of rescue, it is invaluable; because it is, on the part of him who takes it, a complete removal of himself from the sphere of temptation, and so long as he holds himself away from the touch and taste of liquor, he is safe. If the pledge will enable him to do this, then the pledge will save him. But it is well known, from sad experience, that only a few are saved by the pledge. The strength that saves must be something more than the external bond of a promise; it must come from within, and be grounded in a new and changed life, internally as well as externally. If the reformed man, after he takes his pledge, does not endeavor to lead a better moral life—does not keep himself away from old debasing associations—does not try, earnestly and persistently, to become, in all things,

A TRUER, PURER, NOBLER MAN,

then his pledge is only as a hoop, that any over-strain may break, and not an internal bond, holding in integrity all things from the centre to the circumference of his life.

So well is this now understood, that little reliance is had on the pledge in itself, though its use is still general. It is regarded as a first and most important step in the right direction. As the beginning of a true and earnest effort on the part of some unhappy soul to break the bonds of a fearful slavery. But few would think of leaving such a soul to the saving power of the pledge alone. If other help came not, the effort would be, except in rare cases, too surely, all in vain.

The need of something more reliable than a simple pledge has led to other means of reform and cure, each taking character and shape from the peculiar views of those who have adopted them. Inebriate Asylums and Reformatory Homes have been established in various parts of the country, and through their agency many who were once enslaved by drink are being restored to society and good citizenship. In what is popularly known as the "Gospel Temperance" movement, the weakness of the pledge, in itself, is recognized, and, "God being my helper," is declared to be the ultimate and only sure dependence.

It is through this abandonment of all trust in the pledge, beyond a few exceptional cases, that reformatory work rises to its true sphere and level of success. And we shall now endeavor to show what is being done in the work of curing drunkards, as well in asylums and Reformatory Homes, as by the so-called "Gospel" methods. In this we shall, as far as possible, let each of these important agencies speak for itself, explaining its own methods and giving its own results. All are accomplishing good in their special line of action; all are saving men from the curse of drink, and the public needs to be more generally advised of what they are doing.

CHAPTER VIII.

INEBRIATE ASYLUMS.

THE careful observation and study of inebriety by medical men, during the past twenty-five or thirty years, as well in private practice as in hospitals and prisons, has led them to regard it as, in many of its phases, a disease needing wise and careful treatment. To secure such treatment was seen to be almost impossible unless the subject of intemperance could be removed from old associations and influences, and placed under new conditions, in which there would be no enticement to drink, and where the means of moral and physical recovery could be judiciously applied. It was felt that, as a disease, the treatment of drunkenness, while its subject remained in the old atmosphere of temptation, was as difficult, if not impossible, as the treatment of a malarious fever in a miasmatic district. The result of this view was the establishment of Inebriate Asylums for voluntary or enforced seclusion, first in the United States, and afterwards in England and some of her dependencies.

In the beginning, these institutions did not have much favor with the public; and, as the earlier methods of treatment pursued therein were, for the most part, experimental, and based on a limited knowledge of the pathology of drunkenness, the beneficial results were not large. Still, the work went on, and the reports of cures made by the New York State Asylum, at Binghampton, the pioneer of these institutions, were sufficiently encouraging to lead to their establishment in other places; and there are now in this country as many as from twelve to fifteen public and private institutions for the treatment of drunkenness. Of these, the New York State Inebriate Asylum, at Binghamton; the Inebriate Home, at Fort Hamilton, Long Island; and the Home for Incurables, San Francisco, Cal., are the most prominent. At Hartford, Conn., the Walnut Hill Asylum has recently been opened for the treatment of inebriate and opium cases, under the care of Dr. T. D. Crothers. The Pinel Hospital, at Richmond, Va., chartered by the State, in 1876, is for the treatment of nervous and mental diseases, and for the reclamation of inebriates and opium-eaters. In Needham, Mass., is the Appleton Temporary Home, where a considerable number of inebriates are received every year.

Besides these, there are private institutions, in which dypsomaniac patients are received. The methods of treatment differ according to the views and experience of those having charge of these institutions. Up to this time a great deal of the treatment has been experimental; and there is still much difference of opinion among physicians and superintendents in regard to the best means of cure. But, on two important points, all are nearly in agreement. The first is in the necessity for an immediate and

ABSOLUTE WITHDRAWAL OF ALL INTOXICANTS FROM THE PATIENT,

no matter how long he may have used them; and the second in the necessity of his entire abstinence therefrom after leaving the institution. *The cure never places a man back where he was before he became subject to the disease; and he can never, after his recovery, taste even the milder forms of alcoholic beverage without being exposed to the most imminent danger of relapse.*

The great value of an asylum where the victim of intemperance can be placed for a time beyond the reach of alcohol is thus stated by Dr. Carpenter: "Vain is it to recall the motives for a better course of conduct, to one who is already familiar with them all, but is destitute of the will to act upon them; the seclusion of such persons from the reach of alcoholic liquors, for a sufficient length of time to *free the blood from its contamination, to restore the healthful nutrition of the brain and to enable the recovered mental vigor to be wisely directed, seems to afford the only prospect of reformation:* and this cannot be expected to be permanent, unless the patient determinately adopts and steadily acts on the resolution to abstain from that which, *if again indulged in, will be poison, alike to his body and to his mind.*"

In the study of inebriety and the causes leading thereto, much important information has been gathered by the superintendents and physicians connected with these establishments. Dr. D. G. Dodge, late Superintendent of the New York State Inebriate Asylum, read a paper before the American Association for the Cure of Inebriates, in 1876, on "Inebriate Asylums and their Management," in which are given the results of many years of study, observation and experience. Speaking of the causes leading to drunkenness, he says:

"Occupation has a powerful controlling influence in developing or warding off the disease. In-door life in all kinds of business, is a predisposing cause, from the fact that nearly the whole force of the stimulant is concentrated and expended upon the brain and nervous system. A proper amount of out-door exercise, or labor, tends to throw off the stimulus more rapidly through the various functional operations of the system. Occupation of all kinds, mental or muscular, assist the nervous system to retard or resist the action of stimulants—other conditions being equal. Want of employment, or voluntary idleness is the great nursery of this disease.

TOBACCO.

"*The use of tobacco predisposes the system to alcoholism*, and it has an effect upon the brain and nervous system similar to that of alcohol. The use of tobacco, if not prohibited, should be discouraged.

The treatment of inebriates can never be wholly successful until the use of tobacco in all forms is absolutely dispensed with.

"Statistics show that inebriety oftenest prevails between the *ages of thirty and forty-five. The habit seldom culminates until thirty,* the subject to this age generally being a *moderate drinker; later in life the system is unable to endure the strain of a continued course of dissipation.*

"Like all hereditary diseases, intemperance is transmitted from parent to child as much as scrofula, gout or consumption. It observes all the laws in transmitting disease. It sometimes overleaps one generation and appears in the succeeding, or it will miss even the third generation, and then reappear in all its former activity and violence. Hereditary inebriety, like all transmissible diseases, gives the least hope of permanent cure, and temporary relief is all that can generally be reasonably expected.

"Another class possesses an organization which may be termed an alcoholic idiosyncrasy; with them the latent desire for stimulants, if indulged, soon leads to habits of intemperance, and eventually to a morbid appetite, which has all the characteristics of a diseased condition of the system, which the patient, unassisted, is powerless to relieve, since the weakness of will that led to the disease obstructs its removal.

"The second class may be subdivided as follows: First, those who have had healthy and temperate parents, and have been educated and accustomed to good influences, moral and social, but whose temperament and physical constitution are such *that when they once indulge in the use of stimulants, which they find pleasurable, they continue to habitually indulge till they cease to be moderate, and become excessive drinkers. A depraved appetite is established that leads them on slowly, but surely, to destruction.*

"Temperaments have much to do with the formation of the habit of excessive drinking. Those of a nervous temperament are less likely to contract the habit, from the fact that they are acutely sensitive to danger, and avoid it while they have the power of self-control. On the other hand, those of a bilious, sanguine and lymphatic temperament, rush on, unmindful of the present, and soon become slaves to a depraved and morbid appetite, powerless to stay, or even to check their downward course."

As we cannot speak of the treatment pursued in inebriate asylums from personal observation, we know of no better way to give our readers correct impressions on the subject, than to quote still farther from Dr. Dodge. "For a better understanding," he says, "of the requisite discipline demanded in the way of remedial restraint of inebriates, we notice some of the results of chronic inebriation affecting more particularly the brain and nervous system—which, in addition to the necessary medical treatment, necessitates strict discipline to the successful management of these cases.

RESULTS OF CHRONIC INEBRIATION.

"We have *alcoholic epilepsy, alcoholic mania, delirium tremens, tremors, hallucinations, insomnia, vertigo, mental and muscular debility, impairment of vision, mental depression, paralysis, a partial or total loss of self-respect and a departure of the power of self-control.* Many minor difficulties arise from mere functional derangement of the brain and nervous system, which surely and rapidly disappear when the cause is removed."

The general rule, on the reception of a patient, is to cut off at once and altogether the use of alcohol in every form. "More," says the doctor, "can be done by diet and medicine, than can be obtained by a compromise in the moderate use of stimulants for a limited period." It is a mistake, he adds, to suppose "that any special danger arises from stopping the accustomed stimulus. Alcohol is a poison, and we should discontinue its use at once, as it can be done with safety and perfect impunity, except in rare cases."

To secure all the benefits to be derived from medical treatment, "we should have," says Dr. Dodge, "institutions for the reception of inebriates, where total abstinence can be rigidly, but judiciously enforced for a sufficient length of time, to test the curative powers of absolute restraint from all intoxicating drinks. When the craving for stimulants is irresistible, it is useless to make an attempt to reclaim and cure the drunkard, *unless the detention is compulsory*, and there is complete restraint from all spirituous or alcoholic stimulants."

REMOVAL FROM TEMPTATION.

In regard to the compulsory power that should inhere in asylums for the cure of drunkenness, there is little difference of opinion among those who have had experience in their management. They have more faith in time than in medicine, and think it as much the duty of the State to establish asylums for the treatment of drunkenness as for the treatment of insanity. "The length of time necessary to cure inebriation," says Dr. Dodge, "is a very important consideration. A habit covering five, ten, fifteen or twenty years, cannot be expected to be permanently eradicated in a week or a month. The fact that the excessive use of stimulants for a long period of time has caused a radical change, physically, mentally and morally, is not only the strongest possible proof that its entire absence is necessary, but, also, that it requires a liberal allowance of time to effect a return to a normal condition. The shortest period of continuous restraint and treatment, as a general rule, should not be less than six months in the most hopeful cases, and extending from one to two years with the less hopeful, and more especially for the class of periodical drinkers, and those with an hereditary tendency."

A well-directed inebriate asylum not only affords, says the same authority, "effectual removal of the patient from temptations and associations which surrounded him in the outer world, but by precept and example it teaches him that he can gain by his reformation, not the ability to drink moderately and with the least safety, *but the power to abstain altogether.* With the restraint imposed by the institution, and the self-restraint accepted on the part of the patient, are remedial agents from the moment he enters the asylum, growing stronger and more effective day by day, until finally he finds *total abstinence not only possible, but permanent.* With this much gained in the beginning, the asylum is prepared to assist in the cure by all the means and appliances at its command. With the co-operation of the patient, and such medicinal remedies and hygienic and sanitary measures as may be required, the most hopeful results may be confidently looked for.

THE HYGIENIC AND SANITARY MEASURES

consist in total abstinence from all alcoholic beverages; good nourishing diet; well ventilated rooms; pure, bracing air; mental rest, and proper bodily exercise. * * * Every patient should be required to conform to all rules and regulations which have for their object the improvement of his social, moral and religious condition. He must begin a different mode of life, by breaking up former habits and associations; driving from the mind the old companions of an intemperate life; forming new thoughts, new ideas and new and better habits, which necessitates a new life in every respect. This is the aim and object of the rules for the control and government of inebriates. To assist in this work, inebriate institutions should have stated religious services, and all the patients and officers should be required to attend them, unless excused by the medical officer in charge, for sickness, or other sufficient cause."

THE BINGHAMPTON ASYLUM.

Of all the inebriate asylums yet established, the one at Binghampton, New York, has been, so far, the most prominent. It is here that a large part of the experimental work has been done; and here, we believe, that the best results have been obtained. This asylum is a State Institution, and will accommodate one hundred and twenty patients. In all cases preference must be given to "indigent inebriates," who may be sent to the asylum by county officers, who are required to pay seven dollars a week for the medical attendance, board and washing, of each patient so sent. Whenever there are vacancies in the asylum, the superintendent can admit, under special agreement, such private patients as may seek admission, and who, in his opinion, promise reformation.

The building is situated on an eminence two hundred and fifty feet above the Susquehanna River, the scenery stretching far up and down the valley, having features of uncommon beauty and grandeur.

Each patient has a thoroughly warmed and ventilated room, which, from the peculiar situation of the house, commands a wide view of the adjoining country. The tables are supplied with a variety and abundance of good food, suitable in every respect to the wants of the patients, whose tastes and needs are carefully considered. Amusements of various kinds, including billiards, etc., are provided within the building, which afford pleasure and profit to the patients. Out-door pastimes, such as games of ball and croquet, and other invigorating sports, are encouraged and practised. The asylum grounds embrace over four hundred acres, part of which are in a state of cultivation. The remainder diversified in character, and partly consisting of forest.

Gentlemen who desire to place themselves under the care of the asylum, may enter it without any other formality than a compliance with such conditions as may be agreed upon between themselves and the superintendent. The price of admission varies according to location of rooms and attention required. Persons differ so widely in their circumstances and desires, that the scale of prices has been fixed at from ten to twenty-five dollars per week, which includes board, medical attendance, washing, etc. In all cases the price of board for three months must be paid in advance.

From one of the annual reports of this institution now before us, we learn that the number of patients treated during the year was three hundred and thirty-six, of whom one hundred and ninety-eight "were discharged with great hopes of permanent reformation." Fifty-eight were discharged unimproved. The largest number of patients in the asylum at one time was a hundred and five.

SAVING AND REFORMING INFLUENCES.

Of those discharged—two hundred and fifty-six in number—eighty-six were of a nervous temperament, ninety-eight sanguine and seventy-two bilious. In their habits, two hundred and thirty-four were social and twenty-two solitary. Out of the whole number, two hundred and forty-four used tobacco—only twelve being free from its use. Of these, one hundred and sixty had been constant and ninety-six periodical drinkers. Serious affliction, being unfortunate in business, love matters, prosperity, etc., were given as reasons for drinking by one hundred and two of the patients. One hundred and twenty-two had intemperate parents or ancestors. One hundred and forty were married men and one hundred and sixteen single. Their occupations were varied. Merchants, fifty-eight; clerks, thirty-five; lawyers, seventeen; book-keepers, sixteen; manufacturers, eight; bankers and brokers, eight; machinists, seven; mechanics, six; farmers, six; clergymen, five; editors and reporters, five, etc.

In regard to some of the special influences brought to bear upon the patients in this institution, we have the following. It is from a communication (in answer to a letter of inquiry) received by us from Dr. T. D. Crothers, formerly of Binghampton, but now superintendent of the new Walnut Hill Asylum, at Hartford, Connecticut: "You have failed to do us credit," he says, "in supposing that we do not use the spiritual forces in our treatment. We depend largely upon them. We have a regularly-appointed chaplain who lives in the building, and gives his entire time to the religious culture of the patients. Rev. Dr. Bush was with us eight years. He died a few months ago. He was very devoted to his work, and the good he did, both apparent to us and unknown, was beyond estimate. His correspondence was very extensive, and continued for years with patients and their families. He was the counselor and adviser of many persons who did not know him personally, but through patients. I have seen letters to him from patients in all conditions asking counsel, both on secular and spiritual matters; also the most heart-rending appeals and statements of fathers, mothers, wives and children, all of which he religiously answered. He urged that the great duty and obligation of every drunkard was to take care of his body; to build up all the physical, to avoid all danger, and take no risks or perils; that his only help and reliance were on *God and good health;* that with regular living and healthy surroundings, and a mind full of faith and hope in spiritual realities, the disorder would die out. Our new chaplain holds daily service, as usual, and spends much of his time among the patients. He lives in the building, pronounces grace at the table and is personally identified as a power to help men towards recovery. Quite a large number of patients become religious men here. Our work and its influences have a strong tendency this way. I believe in the force of a chaplain whose daily walk is with us; who, by example and precept, can win men to higher thoughts. He is the receptacle of secrets and much of the inner life of patients that physicians do not reach."

In another letter to us, Dr. Crothers says: "Every asylum that I know of is doing good work, and should be aided and encouraged by all means. The time has not come yet, nor the experience or study to any one man or asylum, necessary to build up a system of treatment to the exclusion of all others. We want many years of study by competent men, and the accumulated experience of many asylums before we can understand the first principles of that moral and physical disorder we call drunkenness.

TREATMENT.

"As to the treatment and the agents governing it, we recognize in every drunkard general debility and conditions of nerve and brain exhaustion, and a certain train of exciting causes which always end in drinking. Now, if we can teach these men the 'sources of danger,' and pledge them and point them to a higher power for help, we combine both spiritual and physical means. We believe that little can be expected from spiritual aids, or pledges, or resolves, unless the patient can so build up his physical as to sustain them. Give a man a healthy body and brain-power, and you can build up his spiritual life; but all attempts to cultivate a power that is crushed by diseased forces will be practically useless. Call it a vice or a disease, it matters not, the return to health must be along *the line of natural laws and means.* Some men will not feel any longing for drink unless they get in the centre of excitement, or violate some natural law, or neglect the common means of health. Now, teach them these exciting causes, and build up their health, and the pledge will not be difficult to keep. This asylum is a marvel. It is, to-day, successful. Other asylums are the same, and we feel that we are working in the line of laws that are fixed, though obscure."

DEEPLY INTERESTING CASES.

The records of this institution furnish cases of reform of the most deeply interesting character. Here are a few of them:

Case No. 1. A Southern planter who had become a drunkard was brought to this asylum by his faithful colored man. In his fits of intoxication he fell into the extraordinary delusion that his devoted wife was unfaithful; and so exasperated did he become when seized by this insane delusion, that he often attempted her life. She was at last obliged to keep out of his way whenever he came under the influence of liquor. When sober, his memory of these hallucinations was sufficiently distinct to fill him with sorrow, shame and fear; for he sincerely loved his wife and knew her to be above reproach. After the war, during which he held the position of a general in the Southern army, he became very much reduced in his circumstances, lost heart and gave himself up to drink. The friends of his wife tried to prevail on her to abandon him; but she still clung to her husband, though her life was often in danger from his insane passion. Four years of this dreadful experience, in which she three times received serious personal injuries from his hands, and then the old home was broken up, and he went drifting from place to place, a human ship without a rudder on temptation's stormy sea; his unhappy wife following him, more or less, in secret, and often doing him service and securing his protection. In the spring of 1874, his faithful colored man brought him to the asylum at Binghampton, a perfect wreck. His wife came, also, and for three months boarded near the institution, and, without his knowledge, watched and prayed for him. After a few weeks' residence, the chaplain was able to lead his mind to the consideration of spiritual subjects, and to impress him with the value of religious faith and the power of prayer. He became, at length, deeply interested; read many religious books, and particularly the Bible. At the end of three months his wife came to see him, and their meeting was of a most affecting character. A year later, he left the asylum and went to a Western city, where he now resides—a prosperous and happy man.

CASE No. 2. A clergyman of fortune, position and education lost his daughter, and began to drink in order to drown his sorrow. It was in vain that his wife and friends opposed, remonstrated, implored and persuaded; he drank on, the appetite steadily increasing, until he became its slave. His congregation dismissed him; his wife died of a broken heart; he squandered his fortune; lost his friends, and, at last, became a street reporter for some of the New York papers, through means of which he picked up a scanty living. From bad to worse, he swept down rapidly, and, for some offense committed while drunk, was, at last, sent for three months to the State prison. On coming out, and returning to the city, he became a fish-peddler, but continued to drink desperately. One day he was picked up in the street in a state of dead intoxication and taken to the hospital, where he was recognized by the doctor, who had him sent to Binghampton as a county patient. Here he remained for over a year, submitting himself to the regime, and coming under the salutary influences of the institution, and making an earnest, prayerful and determined effort at reform. At the end of this period he left the asylum to enter upon the duties of a minister in the far

West; and to-day he is the president of a new college, and a devout and earnest man! He attributes his cure to the influence of the late chaplain, Rev. Mr. Bush, and to the new life he was able to lead under the protecting influences and sanitary regulations of the asylum. This is a meagre outline of a very remarkable case.

Case No. 3. A poor farmer's boy acquired, while in the army, an inordinate appetite for drink. He was sent to the New York Inebriate Asylum, but was expelled because he made no effort to reform. Six months afterwards he joined a temperance society, and kept sober for a year; but fell, and was again sent to the asylum. This time he made an earnest effort, and remained at the asylum for seven months, when he was offered a situation in Chicago, which he accepted. For a year he held this place, then relapsed and came back to the asylum, where he stayed for over twelve months. At the end of that time he returned to Chicago and into his old situation. He is now a member of the firm, and an active temperance man, with every prospect of remaining so to the end of his life.

THE CARE AND TREATMENT OF DRUNKARDS.

The subject of the care and treatment of habitual drunkards is attracting more and more attention. They form so large a non-producing, and often vicious and dangerous class of half-insane men, that considerations of public and private weal demand the institution of some effective means for their reformation, control or restraint. Legislative aid has been invoked, and laws submitted and discussed; but, so far, beyond sentences of brief imprisonment in jails, asylums and houses of correction, but little has really been done for the prevention or cure of the worst evil that inflicts our own and other civilized nations. On the subject of every man's "liberty to get drunk," and waste his substance and abuse and beggar his family, the public mind is peculiarly sensitive and singularly averse to restrictive legislation. But a public sentiment favorable to such legislation is steadily gaining ground; and to the formation and growth of this sentiment, many leading and intelligent physicians, both in this country and Great Britain, who have given the subject of drunkenness as a disease long and careful attention, are lending all their influence. It is seen that a man who habitually gets drunk is dangerous to society, and needs control and restraint as much as if he were insane.

LEGISLATIVE CONTROL.

In 1875, a deputation, principally representative of the medical profession, urged upon the British Government the desirability of measures for the control and management of habitual drunkards. On presenting the memorial to the Secretary of State for the Home Department, Sir Thomas Watson, M.D., observed: "That during his very long professional life he had been incredulous respecting the reclamation of habitual drunkards; but his late experience had made him sanguine as to their cure, with a very considerable number of whom excessive drinking indulged in as a vice, developed itself into a most formidable bodily and mental disease."

In the early part of February, 1877, "A Bill to Facilitate the Control and Care of Habitual Drunkards," was introduced into the House of Commons. It is supposed to embody the latest and most practical methods of dealing legally with that class, and is of unusual interest from the fact that it was prepared under the direction of a society for the promotion of legislation for the cure of habitual drunkards, recently organized in London, in which are included some of the most learned, influential and scientific men of the Kingdom.

This bill provides for the establishment of retreats or asylums, public or private, into which drunkards may be admitted on their own application, or to which they may be sent by their friends, and where they can be held by law for a term not exceeding twelve months.

In the State of Connecticut, there is a law which may be regarded as embodying the most advanced legislation on this important subject. The first section is as follows:

"Whenever any person shall have become an habitual drunkard, a dypsomaniac, or so far addicted to the intemperate use of narcotics or stimulants as to have lost the power of self-control, the Court of Probate for the district in which such person resides, or has a legal domicil, shall, on application of a majority of the selectmen of the town where such person resides, or has a legal domicil, or of any relative of such person, make due inquiry, and if it shall find such person to have become an habitual drunkard, or so far addicted to the intemperate use of narcotics or stimulants as to have lost the power of self-control, then said court shall order such person to be taken to some inebriate asylum within this State, for treatment, care and custody, for a term not less than four months, and not more than twelve months; but if said person shall be found to be a dypsomaniac, said term of commitment shall be for the period of three years: *provided, however,* that the Court of Probate shall not in either case make such order without the certificate of at least two respectable practising physicians, after a personal examination, made within one week before the time of said application or said commitment, which certificate shall contain the opinion of said physicians that such person has become, as the case may be, a dypsomaniac, an habitual drunkard, or has, by reason of the intemperate use of narcotics or stimulants, lost the power of self-control, and requires the treatment, care and custody of some inebriate asylum, and shall be subscribed and sworn to by said physicians before an authority empowered to administer oaths."

LOSS TO THE STATE IN NOT ESTABLISHING ASYLUMS.

In a brief article in the *Quarterly Journal of Inebriety*, for 1877, Dr. Dodge thus emphasizes his views of the importance to the State of establishing asylums to which drunkards may be sent for treatment: "Every insane man who is sent to an asylum, is simply removed from doing harm, and well cared for, and rarely comes back to be a producer again. But inebriates (the hopeful class) promise immeasurably more in their recovery. They are, as inebriates, non-producers and centres of disease, bad sanitary and worse moral surroundings. All their career leads down to crime and poverty. The more drunkards, the more courts of law, and almshouses, and insane asylums, and greater the taxes. Statistics show that from fifty to sixty per cent. of crime is due to drunkenness; and we all know how large poverty is due to this cause. Drunkenness is alone responsible for from twenty to twenty-five per cent. of all our insane.

"We assert, and believe it can be proved, that reclaiming the drunkard is a greater gain to the State, practical and immediate, than any other charity.

"It is a low estimate to say it costs every county in the State three hundred dollars yearly to support a drunkard; that is, this amount, and more, is diverted from healthy channels of commerce, and is, practically, lost to the State. At an inebriate asylum, but little over that amount would, in a large majority of cases, restore them as active producers again.

"Figures cannot represent the actual loss to society, nor can we compute the gain from a single case cured and returned to normal life and usefulness. Inebriety is sapping the foundation of our Government, both State and National, and unless we can provide means adequate to check it, we shall leave a legacy of physical, moral and political disease to our descendants, that will ultimately wreck this country. Inebriate asylums will do much to check and relieve this evil."

We conclude this chapter, which is but an imperfect presentation of the work of our inebriate asylums, by a quotation from the *Quarterly Journal of Inebriety*, for September, 1877. This periodical is published under the auspices of "The American Association for the Cure of Inebriates." The editor, Dr. Crothers, says: "We publish in this number, reports of a large number of asylums from all parts of the country, indicating great prosperity and success, notwithstanding the depression of the times. Among the patients received at these asylums, broken-down merchants, bankers, business men, who are inebriates of recent date, and chronic cases that have been moderate drinkers for many years, seem to be more numerous. The explanation is found in the peculiar times in which so many of the business men are ruined, and the discharge of a class of employees whose uncertain habits and want of special fitness for their work make them less valuable. Both of these classes drift to the inebriate asylum, and, if not able to pay, finally go to insane hospitals and disappear.

"Another class of patients seem more prominent this year, namely, the hard-working professional and business men, who formerly went away to Europe, or some watering-place, with a retinue of servants; now they appear at our retreats, spend a few months, and go away much restored. The outlook was never more cheery than at present, the advent of several new asylums, and the increased usefulness of those in existence, with the constant agitation of the subject among medical men at home and abroad, are evidence of great promise for the future. Of the Journal we can only say that, as the organ of the American Association for the Cure of Inebriates, it will represent the broadest principles and studies which the experience of all asylums confirm, and independent of any personal interest, strive to present the subject of inebriety and its treatment in its most comprehensive sense."

CHAPTER IX.

REFORMATORY HOMES.

DIFFERING in some essential particulars from inebriate asylums or hospitals for the cure of drunkenness as a disease, are the institutions called "Homes." Their name indicates their character. It is now about twenty years since the first of these was established. It is located at 41 Waltham Street, Boston, in an elegant and commodious building recently erected, and is called the "Washingtonian Home." The superintendent is Dr. Albert Day. In 1863, another institution of this character came into existence in the city of Chicago. This is also called the "Washingtonian Home." It is situated in West Madison Street, opposite Union Park. The building is large and handsomely fitted up, and has accommodations for over one hundred inmates. Prof. D. Wilkins is the superintendent. In 1872 "The Franklin Reformatory Home," of Philadelphia, was established. It is located at Nos. 911, 913 and 915 Locust Street, in a well-arranged and thoroughly-furnished building, in which all the comforts of a home may be found, and can accommodate over seventy persons. Mr. John Graff is the superintendent.

As we have said, the name of these institutions indicates their character. They are not so much hospitals for the cure of a disease, as homes of refuge and safety, into which the poor inebriate, who has lost or destroyed his own home, with all its good and saving influences, may come and make a new effort, under the most favoring influences, to recover himself.

The success which has attended the work of the three institutions named above, has been of the most gratifying character. In the

WASHINGTONIAN HOME AT BOSTON,

drunkenness has been regarded as a malady, which may be cured through the application of remedial agencies that can be successfully employed only under certain conditions; and these are sought to be secured for the patient. The home and the hospital are, in a certain sense, united. "While we are treating inebriety as a disease, or a pathological condition," says the superintendent, in his last report, "there are those who regard it as a species of wickedness or diabolism, to be removed only by moral agencies. Both of these propositions are true in a certain sense. There is a difference between sin and evil, but the line of demarkation is, as yet, obscure, as much so as the line between the responsibility and irresponsibility of the inebriate."

Doubtless, the good work done in this excellent institution is due, in a large measure, to the moral and religious influences under which the inmates are brought. Nature is quick to repair physical waste and deterioration, when the exciting causes of disease are removed. The diseased body of the drunkard, as soon as it is relieved from the poisoning influence of alcohol, is restored, in a measure, to health. The brain is clear once more, and the moral faculties again able to act with reason and conscience. And here comes in the true work of the Home, which is the restoration of the man to a state of rational self-control; the quickening in his heart of old affections, and the revival of old and better desires and principles.

BENEFICIAL RESULTS.

"Among the beneficial results of our labor," says Dr. Day, "we see our patients developing a higher principle of respect for themselves and their friends. This, to us, is of great interest. We see indications convincing us that the mind, under our treatment, awakens to a consciousness of what it is, and what it is made for. We see man becoming to himself a higher object, and attaining to the conviction of the equal and indestructible of every being. In them we see the dawning of the great principle advocated by us continually, viz., That the individual is not made to be the instrument of others, but to govern himself by an inward law, and to advance towards his proper perfections; that he belongs to himself and to God, and to no human superior. In all our teachings we aim to purify and ennoble the character of our patients by promoting in them true virtue, strong temperance proclivities and a true piety; and to accomplish these ends we endeavor to stimulate their own exertions for a better knowledge of God, and for a determined self-control."

And again he says: "Almost every day we hear from some one who has been with us under treatment, who has been cured. Their struggles had been fierce, and the battle sometimes would seem to be against them; but, at last, they have claimed the victory. In my experience, I have found that so long as the victim of strong drink has the will, feeble as it may be, to put forth his efforts for a better life, and his constant struggle is in the right direction, he is almost sure to regain his will power, and succeed in overcoming the habit. By exercise, the will gains strength. The thorns in the flesh of our spiritual nature will be plucked out, the spiritual life will be developed, and our peace shall flow as the river. This condition we constantly invoke, and by all the means within our reach we try to stimulate the desire for a better life. I am pleased to say our efforts in this direction have not been in vain. For nearly twenty years we have been engaged in this work, and we have now more confidence in the means employed than at any other period. Situated, as we are, in the midst of a great city, with a Christian sympathy constantly active and co-operating with us, no one can remain in the institution without being the recipient of beneficial influences, the effect of which is salutary in the extreme. I am fully satisfied that the 'Washingtonian Home' is greatly indebted to these moral agencies for its success."

The following letter, received by us, from Otis Clapp, who has been for sixteen years president of the "Washingtonian Home," will give the reader a still clearer impression of the workings of that institution. It is in answer to one we wrote, asking for information about the institution in which he had been interested for so many years:

"BOSTON, August 9th, 1877.

"DEAR SIR:—Your letter is received, and I am glad to learn that your mind is directed to the subject of the curse and cure of drunkenness. This is one of the largest of human fields to work in. The 'Washingtonian Home' was commenced in a very humble way, in November, 1857. An act of incorporation was obtained from the State, March 26th, 1859.

"The institution has, therefore, been in existence nearly twenty years. My connection with it has been for eighteen years—sixteen years as president. During the period of its existence the whole number of patients has been five thousand three hundred and forty-eight. Of this number, the superintendent, Dr. Day, estimates the cured at one-half. Of the remainder, it is estimated that one-half, making one-quarter of the whole, are greatly improved.

"You say, 'I take the general ground, and urge it strongly upon the reader that, *without spiritual help—regeneration, in a word—there is, for the confirmed inebriate, but little hope, and no true safety.*'

"In this I fully concur. I believe in using all the agencies —medical, social, moral and religious—to bear upon the patient, and to encourage him to follow the 'straight and narrow way.' With this view, a morning service is held each day; a Sunday evening service at six o'clock, and every Friday evening a meeting, where patients relate their experience, and encourage each other in gaining power over the enemy. I have had much experience and abundant evidence that these meetings are of great value, for the reason that the patients are the principal speakers, and can do more to encourage each other than those outside of their own ranks. These meetings are usually attended by about equal numbers of both sexes, and, with fine music, can be kept up with interest indefinitely.

"It would be, in my judgment, a matter of wide economy for the intelligent citizens of every city, with twenty thousand or more inhabitants, to establish a home, or asylum for inebriates. Let those who favor sobriety in the community, take a part in it, and they will soon learn how to reach the class who needs assistance. A large, old-fashioned house can be leased at small expense, and the means raised by contributions of money and other necessary articles to start. The act of doing this will soon enable those engaged in the work to learn what the wants are, and how to meet them. It is only obeying the command, 'Go out into the highways and hedges and compel them to come in, that my house may be filled.' This is the Master's work, and those who hear this invitation, as well as those who accept it, will share in its blessings.

"Those who cultivate the spirit of 'love to God, and good-will to their fellow-men,' will be surprised to see how much easier it is to *do* these things when they *try*, than when they only *think* about them.

"Much, of course, depends upon the superintendent, who needs to possess those genial qualities which readily win the confidence and good-will of patients, and which he readily turns to account, by encouraging them to use the means which the Creator has given them to co-operate in curing themselves. The means of cure are in the patient's own hands, and it is quite a gift to be able to make him see it."

THE WASHINGTONIAN HOME AT CHICAGO

is on the same plan, in all essential respects, with that of Boston; and the reports show about the same average of cures and beneficial results. How the patient is treated in this Home may be inferred from the following extract from an article on "The Cause, Effect and Cure of Inebriety," from the pen of Prof. D. Wilkins, the superintendent, which appeared in a late number of *The Quarterly Journal of Inebriety*. In answer to the question, How can we best save the poor drunkard, and restore him to his manhood, his family and society, he says:

"Money, friends, relatives and all have forsaken him, his hope blasted, his ambition gone, and he feels that no one has confidence in him, no one cares for him. In this condition he wends his way to an institution of reform, a penniless, homeless, degraded, lost and hopeless drunkard. Here is our subject, how shall we save him? He has come from the squalid dens, and lanes of filth, of misery, of want, of debauchery and death; no home, no sympathy and no kind words have greeted him, perhaps, for years. He is taken to the hospital. A few days pass, and he awakes from the stupidity of drink, and as he opens his eyes, what a change! He looks around, kind and gentle voices welcome him, his bed is clean and soft, the room beautiful, tasteful and pleasant in its arrangements, the superintendent, the physician, the steward and the inmates meet him with a smile and treat him as a brother. He is silent, lost in meditation. Thoughts of other days, of other years, pass through his mind in quick succession as the tears steal gently down his cheeks. He talks thus to himself: 'I am mistaken. *Somebody does care* for the drunkard. And if somebody cares for me, *I ought to care for myself.*' Here reform first commences. In a few days, when free, to some extent, from alcohol, he is admitted to the freedom of the institution. As he enters the reading-room, the library, the amusement, the gymnasium, dining-room and spacious halls, the conviction becomes stronger and stronger that somebody is interested in the inebriate, and he should be interested in himself. Then comes the lessons of the superintendent. He is taught that he cannot be reformed, but that he can reform himself. That God helps those only who help themselves. That he must ignore all boon companions of the cup as associates, all places where liquor is kept and sold, that, in order to reform himself, he must become a reformer, labor for the good of his brother; in short, he must shun every rivulet that leads him into the stream of intemperance, and as a cap-stone which completes the arch, that he must look to Him from whence cometh all grace and power to help in time of need.

"As he converses with those that are strong in experience, listens to the reading of the Holy Scriptures in the morning devotions, joins in the sweet songs of Zion and unites in unison with his brother inmates in saying the Lord's Prayer, as he hears the strong experiences in the public meetings and secret associations of those who have remained firm for one, two, three, and up to ten or fifteen years, little by little his confidence is strengthened, and almost before he is aware, the firm determination is formed and the resolve made, *I will drink no more.* As week after week, and month after month, glides pleasantly away, these resolutions become stronger and stronger, and by thus educating his intellect and strengthening his moral power, the once hopeless, disheartened and helpless one regains his former manhood and lost confidence, and becomes a moral, independent, reformed man. Perhaps the most difficult thing in this work of reform, is to convince our inmates that resolving to stop drinking, or even stopping drinking for the time being, is not reforming. Those admitted, generally, in about two weeks, under the direction of a skillful physician, and the nursing of a faithful steward, recover so as to sleep well and eat heartily, and their wills, seemingly, are as strong as ever. Feeling thus, they often leave the institution, sobered up, not reformed, and when the periodical time arrives, or temptation comes, they have no moral power to resist, and they rush back to habits of intoxication. They forget that the will is like a door on its hinges, with the animal desires, appetites, evil inclinations and passions attached to one side, leading them into trouble and making them unhappy, unless they are held by the strong power of the sense of moral right attached to the other side, and that for years they have been stifling and weakening this power, until its strength is almost, if not entirely, gone, and that the only way they can possibly strengthen it, independent of the grace of God, is by education, moral light and testing it under circumstances so favorable that it will not yield. It took years of disobedience to destroy the moral power, and it will take years of obedience to restore it again. The inebriate must be taught that he can refrain from drink only as he strengthens this moral power, and this requires time and trial. Here is just where we, as superintendents, or reformers, assume great responsibility. To understand just when to test, and how much temptation can be resisted by those under our charge, requires much wisdom and great experience."

From this extract the reader will learn something of the influences which are brought to bear upon the inmates of a home for the reformation of inebriates; and he will see how much reliance is placed on moral and religious agencies.

TESTIMONY OF THE REFORMED.

From the Chicago Home is issued a monthly paper called *The Washingtonian*, devoted to the interest of the institution and to temperance. In this appear many communications from those who are, or have been, inmates. We make a few selections from some of these, which will be read with interest:

"When I came into the Home, mind, memory, hope and energy were shattered. The only animating thought remaining to me was a misty speculation as to where the next drink was to come from. I had a kind of feeble perception that a few days more of the life I was leading must end my earthly career, but I didn't care. As to the 'hereafter'—that might take care of itself; I had no energy to make any provision for it.

"To-day, how different! A new man, utterly defiant of the devil and all 'his works and pomps,' I am ready and eager to take my place once more in the battle of life; atone for the miserable time gone by; to take again the place in the world I had forfeited, bearing ever in my breast the beautiful maxims of the German poet and philosopher, Schiller: 'Look not sorrowfully into the past; it comes not back again. Wisely improve the present; it is thine. Go forth to meet the shadowy future without fear, and with a manly heart.'"

Another writes: "I have been true and faithful to my promise, and have not touched or tampered with the curse since the first morning I entered the Home, ten months ago to-day, and, Mr. Superintendent, I shall never drink again as long as I live. My whole trust and hope is in God, who made me live, move and have my being; and as long as I trust in Him—and which I am thoroughly satisfied I always shall—I will be crowned with success in each and every good effort I make. * * * The day

I reached here, my little ones were out of town, but were telegraphed for at once. They came in the next morning, and, oh! how my heart rejoiced to see they knew and loved me. They came to my arms and threw their little arms around my neck, and hugged and kissed me until I wept with joy. They begged of me never to leave them again, and I never shall. My dear father, mother and all now wish me to stay with them, for they feel I can now be as great a comfort as I once, I might say, was a terror to them. Thank God, I can prove a comfort to them, and my daily life shall be such that they never can do without me. Praises be to God for His goodness and mercy to me, and for showing and guiding me in the straight path, that which leadeth, at last, to an everlasting life with Him and His redeemed in that great and glorious kingdom above."

Another writes, two years after leaving the Home: "In different places where I lived, I was generally a moving spirit in everything of a literary character, and, from a naturally social, convivial disposition, enjoyed the conversation and society of literary men over a glass of beer more than any other attraction that could have been presented. For years, this continued, I, all the time, an active spirit in whatever church I was a member of, and an active worker in whatever I engaged in, thereby always commanding a prominent position wherever I was. Thus matters progressed till I was about twenty-seven, and then I began to realize my position; but, alas, when it was too late. The kindly admonition of friends and my own intelligence began to tell me the story, and then how I struggled for months and months—a naturally sensitive nature only making me worse—till, at last, the conviction forced itself upon me that, for me there was no redemption, that I was bound, hand and foot, perfectly powerless, and then I was forced to accept the fact. My only desire then was to save those dear to me from any knowledge of the truth; for this reason I chose Chicago for my home. Not wishing to take my own life in my hands, I was simply waiting for the moment when, having gone lower and lower, it would, at last, please God to relieve me of my earthly sufferings. Oh! the mental agonies I endured! Too true is it that the drunkard carries his hell around with him. At any moment I was perfectly willing to die, perfectly willing to trust whatever might be before me in the other world, feeling it could be no worse. At last, by God's grace, I was directed to the 'Washingtonian Home,' and there, for the first time, I learned that I could be free; and in this knowledge lies the power of the Home. The Home took hold of me and bade me be a man, and directed me to God for help; and, at the same time, told me to work out my own salvation. Its teachings were not in vain; and to-day I can look up and ask God's blessing on you all for your kind labors. But for that Home, I should, to-day, have been filling a dishonored grave."

And another says: "It is now over five years since I applied to Mr. Drake for admission to the Home. I was then prostrated, both physically and mentally, to that degree that I had scarcely strength to drag myself along, or moral courage enough to look any decent man in the face. I was often assured that to quit whisky would kill me. I thought there was a probability of that; but, on the other hand, there was a certainty that to continue it would kill me. I resolved to make one more effort and die sober, for I never expected to live; had no hope of that. From the day I entered the Home I have been a changed man. The encouragement and counsel I received there, gave me strength to keep the resolution I had formed, and which I have kept to the present moment, viz: TO DRINK NO MORE! Ever since I left Chicago, I have held a respectable position; and now hold the principal position in a house of business, the doors of which I was forbidden to enter six years ago. I do not write this in any spirit of self-laudation, but simply to lay the honor where it belongs—at the door of the 'Washingtonian Home.'"

The following from the "experience" of one of the inmates of the Chicago "Home," will give the reader an idea of the true character of this and similar institutions, and of the way in which those who become inmates are treated. A lady who took an interest in the writer, had said to him, "You had better go to the Washingtonian Home." What followed is thus related:

HOW I WAS TREATED IN THE HOME.

"I looked at her in surprise. Send me to a reformatory? I told her that I did not think that I was sunk so low, or bound so fast in the coils of the 'worm of the still,' that it was necessary for me, a young man not yet entered into the prime of manhood, to be confined in a place designed for the cure of habitual drunkards. I had heard vague stories, but nothing definite concerning the Home, and thought that the question was an insult, but I did not reply to the question. All that night my thoughts would revert to the above question. My life past since I had become a devotee of the 'demon of strong drink,' passed in review before my mind. What had I gained? How improved? What had I obtained by it? And the answer was nothing. Then I asked myself, What had I lost by it? And the answer came to me with crushing force, everything that maketh life desirable. Starting out young in years into the busy highways of the world, with a good fortune, bright prospects and a host of friends to aid and cheer me on, I had lost ALL in my love for strong drink, and at times I thought and felt that I was a modern Ishmael.

"The lady, the next morning, again returned to the attack, and then, not thinking it an insult, but a benefit, to be conferred on me, I yielded a willing acquiescence. That same evening, with a slow step and aching head, I walked up Madison Street towards the Washingtonian Home, with thoughts that I would be considered by the officers of the institution as a sort of a felon, or, if not that, at least something very near akin to the brute, and it was with a sinking heart that I pushed open the main door and ascended the broad, easy stairs to the office. I asked if the superintendent was in, and the gentlemanly clerk at the desk told me that he was, and would be down immediately, meanwhile telling me to be seated. After the lapse of a few minutes, the superintendent, Mr. Wilkins, came into the office, his countenance beaming with benevolence. He took the card that I had brought with me, read it, and, turning round to where I sat, with a genial smile lighting up his countenance, with outstretched hand, greeted me most kindly and introduced me to the gentlemen present. I was dumbfounded, and it was with great difficulty that I restrained myself from shedding tears. It was the very opposite of the reception that I had pictured that I would receive, and I found that I was to be treated as a human being and not as a brute. With a smile, the superintendent addressed me again, and told me to follow him; and it was with a lighter heart and spirits that I ascended the second flight of stairs than the first, I can assure you. I was brought to the steward, who also greeted me most kindly, conversed with me a short time, fixed up some medicine for me and then took me into the hospital. By the word 'hospital,' dear reader, you must not take the usual definition of all that word implies, but in this case, take it as a moderate-sized room with eight or nine beds, covered with snow-white sheets and coverlids, and filled with air of the purest; no sickly smells or suffering pain to offend the most delicate.

"After a most refreshing night's rest—the first that I had had in three or four long, weary months—I arose, and for a few moments could not realize where I was, but memory came back, and I fell on my knees and gave thanks to God that I had fallen into the hands of the 'Good Samaritans.' After breakfast, I went with great diffidence into the common sitting-room, where there was about ten of the inmates sitting smoking, playing checkers, etc. I did not know how I would be received here, but as soon as I entered I was greeted most kindly and told to make myself at home. It seemed as if my cup was full and running over, and for a few moments I could scarcely speak, and I thought that the institution's motto must be founded on the Saviour's command to 'Love one another.'

"The first day I was not allowed to go down to the dining-room, I still being under the care of the hospital steward. The second day I was discharged from the hospital, assigned a most comfortable and cheerful furnished bed-room, and allowed the liberty of the whole building, and the day passed pleasantly. The next morning, at about six, I was awakened by the clangor of a bell shaken by a vigorous arm. Hurriedly dressing, I descended to the wash-room and performed my ablutions, and then waited for the next step. Half an hour having elapsed, the bell was rung a second time, and we all entered what is called the service-room. Shortly after Mr. Wilkins and his family entered; the superintendent read a chapter of the Bible, the inmates sung a hymn, accompanied on the organ by Miss Clara Wilkins; after a short prayer, the inmates marched in single file to the head of the room, where Mr. Wilkins stood, his kind face actually beaming, and with extended hand greeted every individual inmate. After leaving him we marched to the other side of the room, where we also received a cheery 'good morning,' and cordial grasp of the hand from the estimable and motherly wife of the superintendent. To describe one day is sufficient to picture the manner in which the inmates of the Home (and I sincerely believe that 'home' is the right designation for it) pass their time. I have never felt happier or more contented even in my most prosperous days than I have in these few short days that I have been an inmate of the Washingtonian Home."

In this institution, according to the last annual report, two thousand two hundred and fifty-two persons have been treated since it was opened. Of these, one thousand one hundred and eighteen, or over sixty per cent., are said to have remained sober, or nearly so, up to this time. During the last year two hundred and fifty-eight patients were under treatment (one-third free patients). Of these only thirty had relapsed, the others giving great promise of recovery.

The Philadelphia institution, known as the "FRANKLIN REFORMATORY HOME FOR INEBIATES," has been in existence over five years. It was organized in April, 1872. In this institution intemperance is not regarded as a disease, which may be cured through hygienic or medical treatment, but as *a sin, which must be repented of, resisted and overcome through the help of God.* In order to place the inebriate, who honestly desires to reform and lead a better life, under conditions most favorable to this work of inner reformation and true recovery, all the external associations and comforts of a pleasant home are provided, as with the two institutions whose record of good results has just been made. Its administrative work and home-life vary but little from that of the Homes in Boston and Chicago. But it is differenced from them and other institutions which have for their aim the cure of inebriety, in its rejection of the disease theory, and sole reliance on moral and spiritual agencies in the work of saving men from the curse of drink. It says to its inmates, this appetite for drink is not a disease that medicine can cure, or change, or eradicate. New sanitary conditions, removal from temptations, more favorable surroundings, congenial occupation, improved health, a higher self-respect, a sense of honor and responsibility, and the tenderness and strength of love for wife and children, may be powerful enough as motives to hold you always in the future above its enticements. But, trusting in these alone, you can never dwell in complete safety. You need a deeper work of cure than it is possible for you to obtain from any earthly physician. Only God can heal you of this infirmity.

A RELIGIOUS HOME.

While never undervaluing external influences, and always using the best means in their power to make their institution a home in all that the word implies, the managers have sought to make it distinctively something more—*a religious home.* They rely for restoration chiefly on the reforming and regenerating power of Divine grace. Until a man is brought under spiritual influences, they do not regard him as in safety; and the result of their work so far only confirms them in this view. They say, that in almost every case where an inmate has shown himself indifferent, or opposed to the religious influences of the Home, he has, on leaving it, relapsed, after a short period, into intemperance, while the men who have stood firm are those who have sought help from God, and given their lives to His service.

Under this view, which has never been lost sight of from the beginning, in the work of the "Franklin Home," and which is always urged upon those who seek its aid in their efforts to reform their lives, there has come to be in the institution a pervading sentiment favorable to a religions life as the only safe life, and all who are brought within the sphere of its influence soon become impressed with the fact. And it is regarded as one of the most hopeful of signs when the new inmate is drawn into accord with this sentiment, and as a most discouraging one if he sets himself in opposition thereto.

WHO ARE RECEIVED INTO "THE FRANKLIN HOME."

As in other institutions, the managers of this one have had to gain wisdom from experience. They have learned that there is a class of drinking men for whom efforts at recovery are almost useless; and from this class they rarely now take any one into the Home. Men of known vicious or criminal lives are not received. Nor are the friends of such as indulge in an occasional drunken debauch permitted to send them there for temporary seclusion. None are admitted but men of good character, in all but intemperance; and these must be sincere and earnest in their purpose to reform. The capacity of an institution in which the care, and service, and protection of a home can be given, is too small for mere experiment or waste of effort. There are too many who are anxious, through the means offered in a place like this, to break the chains of a debasing habit, and get back their lost manhood once more, to waste effort on the evil-minded and morally depraved, who only seek a temporary asylum and the opportunity for partial recovery, but with no purpose of becoming better men and better citizens. Apart from the fruitlessness of all attempts to permanently restore such men to sobriety, it has been found that their presence in the Home has had an injurious effect; some having been retarded in recovery through their influence, and others led away into vicious courses.

There is a chapel in the building, capable of holding over two hundred person In this, Divine worship is held every Sunday afternoon. A minister from some one of the churches is usually in attendance to preach and conduct the services. It rarely happens that the chapel is not well filled with present and former inmates of the Home, their wives, children and friends. Every evening, at half-past nine o'clock, there is family prayer in the chapel, and every Sunday afternoon the president, Mr. S. P. Godwin, has a class for Bible study and instruction in the same place. On Tuesday evenings there is a conversational temperance meeting; and on Thursday evening of each week the Godwin Association, organized for mutual help and encouragement, holds a meeting in the chapel.

USE OF TOBACCO DISCOURAGED.

The attending physician, Dr. Robert P. Harris, having given much thought and observation to the effects of tobacco on the physical system, and its connection with inebriety, discourages its use among the inmates, doing all in his power, by advice and admonition, to lead them to abandon a habit that not only disturbs and weakens the nervous forces, but too often produces that very condition of nervous exhaustion which leads the sufferer to resort to stimulation. In many cases where men, after leaving the "Home," have stood firm for a longer or shorter period of time, and then, relapsing into intemperance, have again sought its help in a new effort at reformation, he has been able to find the cause of their fall in an excessive use of tobacco.

Dr. Harris is well assured, from a long study of the connection between the use of tobacco and alcohol, that, in a very large number of cases tobacco has produced the nervous condition which led to inebriety. And he is satisfied that, if men who are seeking to break away from the slavery of drink, will give up their tobacco and their whisky at the same time, they will find the work easier, and their ability to stand by their good resolutions, far greater. See the next chapter for a clear and concise statement, from the pen of Dr. Harris, of the effects of tobacco, and the obstacles its use throws in the way of men who are trying to reform.

WHAT HAS BEEN ACCOMPLISHED.

The results of the work done in this "Home" are of the most satisfactory kind. From the fifth annual report, we learn that there have been received into the Home, since its commencement, seven hundred and forty-one persons. Of these, the report gives three hundred and fifty-four as reformed, and one hundred and three as benefited. Two hundred and ninety-seven were free patients.

WOMAN'S WORK IN THE HOME.

In the management of this Home there is, beside the board of directors, an auxiliary board of twenty-six lady managers, who supervise the work of the Home, and see to its orderly condition and the comfort of the inmates. Through visiting and relief committees the families of such of the inmates as need temporary care and assistance are seen, and such help and counsel given as may be required. An extract or two from the reports of this auxiliary board will not only give an idea of the religious influences of the institution, but of what is being done by the woman's branch of the work. Says the secretary, Mrs. E. M. Gregory, in her last annual report:

"The religious influence exerted by this institution by means of its Sunday evening services, its Bible class and its frequent temperance meetings, which are cordially open to all, is silently, but, we think, surely making itself felt among those brought within its reach, and establishing the highest and strongest bond among those whose natural ties are often unhappily severed by intemperance. We find whole families, long unused to any religious observance, now *regularly, for years*, accompanying the husband and father to this place of worship, and joining devoutly in the exercises.

"Especial emphasis is laid upon the doctrine that the only foundation for a thorough, enduring reformation is found in a radical change of heart, a preparation for the future life by a conscientious, persistent effort to lead a Christ-like life here.

"One result of this teaching is found in the fact that several of the inmates, not in the first pleasant excitement of their rescue from the immediate horrors of their condition, but after long and faithful observance of their pledge and constant attendance upon the religious instruction of the Home, have voluntarily and with solemn resolve united themselves to some Christian church, and are devoting a large share of their time and means to the work of bringing in their old companions to share this great salvation. When, in our visits among their families, we hear of those who formerly spent all their earnings at the saloon, bringing nothing but distress and terror into their homes, now walking the streets all day in search of work, without dinner themselves, because the 'wife and children need what little there is in the house;' and another, not only denying himself a reasonable share of the scanty food, but nursing a sick wife and taking entire care of the children and house, hastening out, when relieved awhile by a kindly neighbor, to do '*anything* to bring in a little money'—when we see changes like these, accompanied by patience and cheerfulness, and a growing sense of personal responsibility, we thankfully accept them as proofs of the genuineness of the work and hopefully look for its continuance."

TOUCHING INCIDENTS.

In a previous report, speaking of the visits made to the families of inmates, she says:

"In no case has a visit ever been received without expression of absolute pleasure, and especially gratitude, for 'what the Home has done for me and mine.'

"Although, unhappily, there are instances of men having, through stress of temptation, violated their pledges, it is believed that not one case has occurred of a family, once brought together through the influence of the Home, again being separated by the return to intemperance of the husband and father, and the results of their faithfulness are to be seen in the growing comfort and happiness of those dependent on them.

"An aged mother, not only bowed down with the weight of seventy years, but heart-sick with the 'hope deferred' of ever finding her intemperate son, heard of him at last, as rescued by the Home; and, being brought to the Sunday and evening services, met him there, 'clothed and in his right mind.' The tears streamed down her face, as she said: 'That man is forty years old, and I've been a widow ever since he was a baby, and I've wept over him often and often, and *to-day* I've shed tears enough to bathe him from head to foot, but, oh! thank the Lord! *these* are such *happy* tears!'

"Said one wife: 'Some days, these hard times, we have enough to eat, and some days we don't; but *all* the time I'm just as happy as I can be!

"'I wish you could see my children run, laughing, to the door when their father comes home. Oh! he is *another* man from what he was a year ago; he is so happy at home with us now, and always so patient and kind!

"'Do tell us if there isn't something—if it is ever so little—that we women can do for the Home; we *never* can forget what it has done for us!'

"Such words, heard again and again with every variety of expression, attests the sincerity of those who, in widely differing circumstances, perhaps, have yet this common bond, that through this instrumentality, they are rejoicing over a husband, a father, a son, 'which was dead, and is alive—was lost, and is found.'

"Surely, such proof of the intrinsic worth of a work like this, is beyond all expression—full of comfort and encouragement to persevere."

Again: "Through their instrumentality families long alienated and separated have been happily brought together. This branch of the ladies' work has been peculiarly blest; and their reward is rich in witnessing not only homes made happier through their labors, but hearts so melted by their personal kindness, and by the Gospel message which they carry, that husbands and wives, convicted of the sinfulness of their neglect of the great salvation, come forward to declare themselves soldiers of the cross, and unite with the Christian church."

THE TESTIMONY OF INMATES.

As the value of this and similar institutions is best seen in what they have done and are doing, we give two extracts from letters received from men who have been reformed through the agency of the "Home" in Philadelphia. In the first, the writer says:

"It has now been nearly two years since I left the Franklin Home. I had been a drinking man ten years, and it got such a hold on me that I could not resist taking it. I had tried a number of times to reform, and at one time, was in the Dashaway's Home, in California, where they steep everything in liquor, but when I came out I still had the desire to drink, and only kept from it for nine months. I again commenced, and kept sinking lower and lower, till I lost my friends, and felt there was no hope for me. On the 31st day of May, 1873, I came to the Franklin Home, and have never tasted intoxicating liquor since, which is the longest time I was ever without it since I commenced to drink. I feel now that I will never drink again, as I do not associate with drinking men, or go to places where liquor is sold. It was so different at the Home from anything I had ever met or heard of, that I went away with more strength to resist than ever before. When I came to the Home I could not get a position in Philadelphia, nobody having confidence in me. Since then I have been engaged as foreman in a manufacturing establishment, by the very man that had discharged me several times for drinking, and have been with him a year. I feel more happy and contented now than any time in ten years past, and if I had a friend who I found this was taking hold of, I would bring him to the Home, for I believe any one that is sincere can be reformed, and I would recommend any man that needs and desires to reform to go to the Home, as I did."

AFTER FIVE YEARS.

Writing to Mr. Samuel P. Godwin, President of the Franklin Home, an old inmate, five years after his reformation, says: "I received your kind letter and recognized in it the challenge of the ever-watchful sentinel, 'How goes the night, brother?' I answer back, 'All is well.' I am delighted to hear of the continued success of 'my second mother,' the Home, and the Association, my brothers; and I thank God, who is encouraging you all in your efforts for fallen men, by showing you the ripening fruits of your labor—efforts and labors that are inspired by a love of God that enables you to see in every fallen man the soul made like unto *His* own image. The Home and all its workers, its principles, the endless and untiring efforts made, challenge the wonder and admiration of every Christian heart. Its grand results will admit of but one explanation, that 'It is God's work.' We, the reclaimed, can never give expression to the grateful emotions of our hearts. We can only let our lives be its best eulogy. We hope to vindicate in the future, as we have in the past, (by adhering to its principles) the great Christian truth, the grace of God is all-powerful, all-saving. *Oh! what has not the Home done for us all!* It sought us amid temptations, misery and sorrow, and took us into its warm and fond embrace, clearing away the debris that intemperance and misfortune had piled up, tearing down all false theories of disease and seizing our convictions. It reached down into our hearts by its admirable practical mode of imparting its principles, impressing all its lessons with the examples of living, active men, who, through its aid, accepting its teachings and practicing them, have become reformed men—in a word, conquerors of self. By its love, fostering care and ever-watchful solicitude for us, it has awakened the lessons of love and faith learned at a dear mother's knee in childhood, which, if forgotten for a time, were never entirely dead, and required but just such an influence to warm them into life. It enables me to say to you now, at the end of five years, I have been a total abstinence man for that time, and by and with the help of God, I will die that."

But enough has been educed to show the importance of this and other "Homes" for the recovery of inebriates, and to direct public attention to their great value. Those already established should be liberally sustained by the communities in which they are located, and similar institutions should be organized and put in operation in all the larger cities of the Union. Thousands of outcast, helpless, perishing men, who, but for the fatal habits they have acquired, would be good and useful citizens, might, if this were done, be every year restored to themselves, their families and to society. If we cannot, as yet, stay the curse that is upon our land, let us do all in our power to heal what has been hurt, and to restore what has been lost.

In every truly reformed man, the temperance cause gains a new and valuable recruit. The great army that is to do successful battle with the destroying enemy that is abroad in the land, will come chiefly from the ranks of those who have felt the crush of his iron heel. So we gain strength with every prisoner that is rescued from the enemy; for every such rescued man will hate this enemy with an undying hatred, and so long as he maintains his integrity, stand fronting him in the field.

Dr. Harris, the attending physician of the "Franklin Reformatory Home," whose long experience and careful observation enable him to speak intelligently as to the causes which lead to relapses among reformed men, has kindly furnished us with the following suggestions as to the dangers that beset their way. The doctor has done a good service in this. To be forewarned is to be forearmed. We are also indebted to him for the chapter on "Tobacco as an Incitant to the Use of Alcoholic Stimulant," which immediately follows this one, and which was especially prepared by him for the present volume.

DANGERS THAT BESET THE REFORMED INEBRIATE.

BY DR. R. P. HARRIS.

"*Come, take a drink.*"—How pernicious is this treating generosity of the inebriate, and how important to the reformed to be firm in declining his invitation. To hesitate, is, in most cases, to yield.

Old companions.—These should be avoided, and made to understand that their company is not congenial; and new and safe ones should be selected.

Attacks of sickness.—A quondam inebriate should never employ a physician who drinks, and should always tell his medical attendant that he cannot take any medicine containing alcohol. It is very unsafe to resort to essence of ginger, paregoric, spirits of lavender or burnt brandy, and friends very injudiciously, sometimes, recommend remedies that are dangerous in the extreme. We saw one man driven into insanity by his employer recommending him a preparation of rhubarb, in Jamaica spirits, which he took with many misgivings, because, six years before he had been a drunkard. The old appetite was revived in full force at once. Diarrhœa can be much better treated without tinctures and essences than with them, as proved by the large experience of the Franklin Home, where they are never prescribed.

Bad company of either sex.—Remember what is said of the strange woman in Proverbs v., 3–12; and the advice given in the first Psalm. Lust has driven to drunkenness and death many a promising case of reform.

Entering a tavern.—It is never safe to buy a cigar, take a glass of lemonade, eat a plate of oysters or even drink water at a bar where liquors are sold. The temptation, and revival of old associations, are too much for weak human nature to withstand.

Politics, military organizations, etc.—Many a man has been made a drunkard by the war, or by becoming an active politician. Associations of men leading to excitement of any kind stimulate them to invite each other to drink as a social custom. Former inebriates should avoid all forms of excitement. Said a former politician, who has not drank for five years: "If I was to go back to politics, and allow matters to take their natural course, I should soon drift again into drunkenness."

"*Idleness,*" says the French proverb, "is the mother of all vices;" hence the advantage and importance of being actively employed.

Working in communities.—There are no men more inclined to drunkenness than shoemakers, hatters and those in machine shops. Shoemakers are especially difficult to reform, as they incite each other to drink, and club together and send out for beer or whisky.

Use of excessive quantities of pepper, mustard and horse-radish.—No person can use biting condiments to the same degree as drunkards; and reformed men must largely moderate their allowance, if they expect to keep their appetite under for something stronger. Tavern-keepers understand that salt and peppery articles, furnished gratis for lunch, will pay back principal and profit in the amount they induce men to drink.

Loss of money or death in the family.—These are among the most severe of all the trials to be encountered by the reformed drunkard. Hazardous ventures in stocks or business are dangerous in the extreme. Without the grace of God in the heart, and the strength that it gives in times of depression of spirits under severe trial, there are few reformed men who can bear, with any safety, the loss of a wife or very dear child. Thousands who have, for the time, abandoned the habit have returned to it to drown, in unconsciousness, their feeling of loss; hence the great and vital importance of an entire change of heart to enable a man to go to his faith for consolation, and to look to God for help in times of trial and temptation.

BOYHOOD.
The First Step.

YOUTH.
The Second Step.

MANHOOD.
A Confirmed Drunkard.

OLD AGE.
A Total Wreck.

CHAPTER X.

TOBACCO AS AN INCITANT TO THE USE OF ALCOHOLIC STIMULANTS, AND AN OBSTACLE IN THE WAY OF A PERMANENT REFORMATION.

BY DR. R. P. HARRIS, PHYSICIAN OF THE "FRANKLIN REFORMATORY HOME."

WHEN we consider the almost universal use of tobacco, especially in the form of smoking, among our male population, it is not to be wondered at that this powerful poison has come to be regarded as an innocent and almost necessary vegetable production, not to be used as food exactly, but greatly allied to it as an article of daily consumption. Few stop to reason about its properties or effects; they remember, perhaps, how sick they were made by the first chew or smoke, but this having long passed, believe that as their systems have become accustomed, *apparently*, to the poison, it cannot be doing them any real injury. When we reflect that tobacco contains from one to nearly seven per cent. of *nicotine*—one of the most powerful vegetable poisons known—a few drops of which are sufficient to destroy life, it is not difficult to perceive that this faith in the *innocence* begotten of use must be fallacious. We have met with instances where the poisonous effects of tobacco were manifest after every smoke, even where the attempt to accustom the system to its use had been persevered in for many years; and yet the men never realized what was the matter with them, until they had, under medical advice, ceased to use the drug.

Before the discovery of anæsthetics, tobacco was used as a remedy to produce relaxation in cases of strangulated hernia; and although very cautiously administered in the form of tea, or smoke per rectum, proved fatal in many instances. As little as twelve grains in six ounces of water having thus acted; and from half a drachm to two drachms in a number of instances. When men chew as high as a pound and a quarter of strong navy tobacco a week, or three packages of fine-cut in a day, it must certainly tell upon them sooner or later; or even in much less quantity.

If men used tobacco in moderation, there would be much less objection to it, if it was not so intimately

ASSOCIATED WITH THE HABIT OF DRINKING.

This is recognized by the trade, in the fact that we see many tobacco stores as the entrance to drinking saloons. Ninety-three per cent. of the men who have been admitted to the Franklin Reformatory Home used tobacco, and eighty per cent. of them chewed it. There may be possibly as high as ninety-three per cent. of male adults who smoke, but eighty per cent. of chewers is undoubtedly a large proport..on as compared with those in the same ranks of society who do not drink.

Although the poisonous symptoms of tobacco are, in a great degree, the same in different persons at the inception of the habit, the effects vary materially in after years according to the quantity and variety used, the form employed and the habits and temperament of the user. One man will chew a paper a week, another four, many use one a day, and a few from one and a half to three a day, besides smoking. Occasionally, but very rarely, we find a man who limits himself to one cigar a day, a number allow themselves but three, but of later years even these are moderate compared with those who use eight, ten or more.

There are many men who, for years, preserve a robust, hale appearance under both tobacco and whisky, who are, notwithstanding their apparent health, steadily laying the foundation of diseased heart, or

DERANGEMENT OF THE DIGESTIVE ORGANS

or nervous system from the former, or an organic fatal disease of the liver or kidneys from the latter.

Healthy-looking men are often rejected by examiners of life insurance companies because of irregular and intermittent action of the heart from tobacco; and equally robust subjects are forced to abandon the habit because of tremors, vertigo or a peculiar form of dyspepsia. We have known men who died from the use of tobacco, and others who met a like fate from whisky, who were never fully in the state denominated drunk. Men may earn a hobnail liver and dropsy by the constant, steady use of alcoholic drink taken systematically, so as always to keep within the limits of intoxication; or they may, in the same way, get a diabetes or Bright's disease.

Abundant testimony in regard to the effects of tobacco in creating an appetite for strong drink has been given by the inmates of the Franklin Home. In a few exceptional cases the use of tobacco does not appear to create any sense of thirst; and this is specially the case with the smokers who do not spit when smoking. Some men seem to be free from any alcoholic craving when using tobacco, and say that when they commence to drink they give up the drug for the time being. These are exceptional cases, for excess in drinking generally leads to an excess in the use of tobacco, often to double the amount ordinarily employed. We have often been told by moderate drinkers, that they frequently

FELT A DESIRE FOR A LITTLE WHISKY AFTER A SMOKE,

and they have confessed that they were only saved from a habit of drinking to excess by the fact that they had no innate fondness for alcoholic stimulation. Unfortunately, there is a large and increasing class of men who, finding that water does not, but that alcohol does, relieve the dryness of throat and diseased thirst resulting from tobacco, are led, little by little, into the habit of using whisky to excess. Such men, after, it may be, a long abstinence, are not unfrequently led back into their old habits by an attack of nervousness, resulting from a temporary excessive use of tobacco, and a feeling that all that is wanting to relieve this is a glass of whisky, which being taken, at once determines a debauch of long or short duration, according to the habits and character of the party. Many a *so-called periodical drinker* fixes the return of his period by an act of this kind, and with such cases it is all-important to their permanent reformation, that they should cease entirely and forever from the use of tobacco. We have, in a few instances, prevailed upon men to do this, but in a large majority of cases, where they have admitted the connection between the two habits, in their own person, or volunteered to tell how much tobacco had acted in forming and keeping up their appetite for whisky, they have failed in being able to sum up sufficient resolution to abandon the use of the drug, saying that they felt the importance of the step, and would be glad to be able to give it up, but that the habit was

TEN TIMES AS DIFFICULT TO CONQUER AS THAT OF WHISKY-DRINKING.

All that we have been able to accomplish in such cases has been to check the excessive use. We have repeatedly assured men, after a careful examination of their peculiar cases, that they would certainly drink again unless they gave up their tobacco, and have seen this opinion verified, because they took no heed to the warning. We have also been gratified in a few instances by hearing a man say that he felt confident that he could never have accomplished his reformation as he had done, if he had not taken the advice given him about abandoning his tobacco. In contrast with the men of weak purpose, we have to admire one who had resolution enough to break off the three habits of opium-eating, whisky-drinking and tobacco-chewing—no trifling matter—when the first was of ten and the last of more than thirty years' duration.

We have been repeatedly asked which was the most injurious, smoking or chewing, and have replied, that everything depended upon the amount of nicotine absorbed in the process, and the loss to the system in the saliva spit out. Men have died from the direct effect of excessive smoking, and quite recently a death in a child was reported from the result of blowing soap-bubbles with an old wooden pipe. We have known a little boy to vomit from drawing air a few times through the empty meerschaum pipe of his German teacher. The smoking of two pipes as the first essay, very nearly caused the death of a young man, whose case was reported by Dr. Marshall Hall.

The least poisonous tobaccos are those of Syria and Turkey, but the cigarettes made of them in the

East and imported into this country are said to be impregnated with opium. Virginia tobacco, for the pipe or chewing, contains a large percentage of nicotine, and the former is often impregnated with foreign matters, recognizable by the choking effect of the smoke when inhaled, or by the removal of the epithelium (outer skin) of the tongue at the point under the end of the pipe-stem.

If we fail in our efforts to reform the tobacco habit, the next best thing to do, is to show men what the nature and capabilities of the poison are, and endeavor to persuade them to use the milder varieties and in a moderate quantity.

ONE OF THE GREAT CURSES OF THE RISING GENERATION

is the passion for imitating and acquiring the evil habits of men, under an impression that it hastens their approach to manhood. Weak, frail, delicate boys, with inherited tendencies to disease, who should, by all means, never use tobacco, or anything injurious, are often as obstinately bent upon learning to smoke, in spite of medical advice, as those in whom a moderate use would be far less objectionable. A recent observer, in examining into the cases of thirty-eight boys who had formed the habit of using tobacco, found that twenty-seven of them had also a fondness for alcoholic stimulants. A large proportion of the Franklin Home inmates attribute their habit of drinking to the effects of company; many commenced in the army, and many were induced to drink at first by invitation. If smoking was a solitary habit, it would be less likely to lead to drinking; but the same companionship, and habits of treating prevail, as in the saloon, and the step from the *estaminet* to the bar-room under invitation, is an easy one, where the diseased thirst, so often induced by tobacco, favors the movement to treat.

We have no prejudice against tobacco, other than what would naturally arise in the mind from a careful examination of the effects of the poison in hundreds of cases. We have seen large, hale-looking men forced in time to abandon, although very reluctantly, the use of tobacco in every form; and the most bitter enemy we have ever met to the *vile weed*, as he termed it, was a physician, who had been forced to give up chewing on account of the state of his heart, after years of indulgence. We have seen many such instances, and, in one case, the abandonment of the habit entirely cured a dyspepsia of twenty-eight years' standing.

CHAPTER XI.

THE WOMAN'S CRUSADE.

FOR every one saved through the agency of inebriate asylums and reformatory homes, hundreds are lost and hundreds added yearly to the great army of drunkards. Good and useful as such institutions are, they do not meet the desperate exigencies of the case. Something of wider reach and quicker application is demanded. What shall it be? In prohibition many look for the means by which the curse of drunkenness is to be abated. But, while we wait for a public sentiment strong enough to determine legislation, sixty thousand unhappy beings are yearly consigned to drunkards' graves.

What have temperance men accomplished in the fifty years during which they have so earnestly opposed the drinking usages of society and the traffic in alcoholic drinks? And what have they done for the prevention and cure of drunkenness? In limiting the use of intoxicants, in restricting the liquor traffic and in giving a right direction to public sentiment, they have done a great and good work; but their efforts to reclaim the fallen drunkard have met with sad discouragements. In the work of prevention, much has been accomplished; in the work of cure, alas! how little. The appetite once formed, and the unhappy victim finds himself under the control of a power from which he can rarely get free. Pledges, new associations, better and more favorable surroundings, all are tried, and many are saved; but the number of the saved are few in comparison with those who, after a season of sobriety, fall back into their old ways.

In all these many years of untiring efforts to lift up and save the fallen, what sad disappointments have met our earnest and devoted temperance workers. From how many fields, which seemed full of a rich promise, have they gathered only a meagre harvest. But still they have worked on, gaining strength from defeat and disappointment; for they knew that the cause in which they were engaged was the cause of God and humanity, and that in the end it must prevail.

Meantime, the bitter, half-despairing cry, "O Lord, how long!" was going up from the lips of broken-hearted wives and mothers all over the land, and year by year this cry grew deeper and more desperate. All hope in man was failing from their hearts. They saw restrictive legislation here and there, and even prohibition; but, except in a few cases, no removal of the curse; for behind law, usage, prejudice, interest and appetite the traffic stood intrenched and held its seat of power.

At last, in the waning years of the first century of our nation's existence, their failing hope in man died utterly, and with another and deeper and more despairing cry, the women of our land sent up their voices to God. Not now saying "O Lord, how long!" but "Lord, come to our help against the mighty!"

What followed is history. The first result of this utter abandonment of all hope in moral suasion or legal force, and of a turning to God in prayer and faith, was that strange, intense, impulsive movement known as the "Woman's Crusade."

BEGINNING OF THE CRUSADE.

Let us briefly give the story of its initiation late in the month of December, 1873. Dr. Dio Lewis, in a lecture which he had been engaged to deliver at Hillsboro, Ohio, related how, forty years before, his pious mother, the wife of a drunkard, who was struggling to feed, clothe and educate her five helpless children, went, with other women who had a similar sorrow with her own, to the tavern-keeper who sold their husbands drink, and, kneeling down in his bar-room, prayed with and for him, and besought him to abandon a business that was cursing his neighbors and bringing want and suffering into their homes. Their prayers and entreaties prevailed. After telling this story of his mother, the lecturer asked all the women present who were willing to follow her example to rise, and in response, nearly the entire audience arose. A meeting was then called for the next morning, to be held in the Presbyterian church.

Dr. Lewis was a guest at the old mansion of Ex-Governor Trimble, father of Mrs. E. J. Thompson, a most cultivated, devoted Christian woman, mother of eight children. She was not present at the lecture, but "prepared," as she writes, "as those who watch for the morning, for the first gray light upon this dark night of sorrow. Few comments were made in our house," she continues, "upon this new line of policy until after breakfast the next morning, when, just as we gathered about the hearth-stone, my daughter Mary said, very gently: 'Mother, will you go the meeting this morning?' Hesitatingly I replied: 'I don't know yet what I shall do.' My husband, fully appreciating the responsibility of the moment, said: 'Children, let us leave your mother alone; for you know where she goes with all vexed questions;' and pointing to the old family Bible, left the room. The awful responsibility of the step that I must needs next take was wonderfully relieved by thought of the 'cloudy pillar' and 'parted waters' of the past; hence, with confidence, I was about turning my eye of faith 'up to the hills,' from whence had come my help, when, in response to a gentle tap at my door, I met my dear Mary, who, with her Bible in hand and tearful eyes, said: 'Mother, I opened to Psalm cxlvi., and I believe it is for you.' She withdrew and I sat down to read the wonderful message from God. As I read what I had so often read before, the Spirit so strangely 'took of the things of God,' and showed me new meanings, I no longer hesitated, but, in the strength thus imparted, started to the scene of action.

"Upon entering the church, I was startled to find myself chosen as leader. The old Bible was taken down from the desk, and Psalm cxlvi. read. Mrs. General McDowell, by request, led in prayer, and, although she had never before heard her own voice in a public prayer, on this occasion 'the tongue of fire' sat upon her, and all were deeply affected. Mrs. Cowden, our Methodist minister's wife, was then requested to sing to a familiar air—

"'Give to the winds thy fears!
  Hope, and be undismayed;
God hears thy sighs and counts thy tears:
  He will lift up thy head.'

And while thus engaged, the women (seventy-five in number) fell in line, two and two, and proceeded first to the drug stores and then to the hotels and saloons."

Thus began this memorable Crusade, which was maintained in Hillsboro for over six months, during which time the saloons were visited almost daily.

Within two days, the women of Washington Court-House, a neighboring town, felt the inspiration of their sisters, and inaugurated the movement there. A description of what was done at this place will afford the reader a clear impression of the way in which the "Crusaders" worked, and the results that followed their efforts. We quote from the account given by Mrs. M. V. Ustick:

"After an hour of prayer, forty-four women filed slowly and solemnly down the aisle and started forth upon their strange mission, with fear and trembling, while the male portion of the audience remained at church to pray from the success of this new undertaking; the tolling of the church-bell keeping time to the solemn march of the women, as they wended their way to the first drug store on the list (the number of places within the city limits where intoxicating drinks were sold was fourteen—eleven saloons and three drug stores). Here, as in every place, they entered singing, every woman taking up the sacred strain as she crossed the threshold. This was followed by the reading of the appeal and prayer, and then earnest pleading to desist from their soul-destroying traffic and to sign the dealers' pledge. Thus, all the day long, going from place to place, without stopping even for dinner or lunch, till five o'clock, meeting with no marked success; but invariably courtesy was extended to them.

"The next day an increased number of women went forth, leaving the men in the church to pray all day long. On this day the contest really began, and at the first place the doors were found locked. With hearts full of compassion, the women knelt in the snow upon the pavement to plead for the Divine influence upon the heart of the liquor-dealer, and there held their first street prayer-meeting. The Sabbath was devoted to a union mass-meeting. Monday, December 29th, is one long to be remembered in Washington as the day on which occurred the first surrender ever made by a liquor-dealer of his stock of liquors of every kind and variety to the women, in answer to their prayers and entreaties, and by them poured into the street. Nearly a thousand men, women and children witnessed the mingling of beer, ale, wine and whisky, as they filled the gutters and were drunk up by the earth, while bells were ringing, men and boys shouting, and women singing and praying to God, who had given the victory.

"On the fourth day, the campaign reached its height; the town being filled with visitors from all parts of the country and adjoining villages. Another public surrender and another pouring into the street of a larger stock of liquors than on the day before, and more intense excitement and enthusiasm. In eight days all the saloons, eleven in number, had been closed, and the three drug stores pledged to sell only on prescription.

"Early in the third week the discouraging intelligence came that a new man had taken out license to sell liquor in one of the deserted saloons, and that he was backed by a whisky house in Cincinnati to the amount of five thousand dollars to break down this movement. On Wednesday, 14th of January, the whisky was unloaded at his room. About forty women were on the ground and followed the liquor in, and remained holding an uninterrupted prayer-meeting all day and until eleven o'clock at night. The next day—bitterly cold—was spent in the same place and manner, without fire or chairs, two hours of that time the women being locked in, while the proprietor was off attending a trial. On the following day, the coldest of the winter of 1874, the women were locked out, and remained on the street holding religious services all day long. Next morning a tabernacle was built in the street just in front of the house, and was occupied for the double purpose of watching and praying through the day; but before night the sheriff closed the saloon, and the proprietor surrendered. A short time afterwards, on a dying bed, this four-day's liquor-dealer sent for some of these women, telling them their songs and prayers had never ceased to ring in his ears, and urging them to pray again in his behalf; so he passed away."

From this beginning the new temperance movement increased and spread with a marvelous rapidity. The incidents attendant on the progress of the "Crusade" were often of a novel and exciting character. Such an interference with their business was not to be tolerated by the liquor men; and they soon began to organize for defense and retaliation. They not only had the law on their side, but in many cases, the administrators of the law. Yet it often happened, in consequence of their reckless violations of statutes made to limit and regulate the traffic, that dealers found themselves without standing in the courts, or entangled in the meshes of the very laws they had invoked for protection.

In the smaller towns the movement was, for a time, almost irresistible; and in many of them the drink traffic ceased altogether. But when it struck the larger cities, it met with impediments, against which it beat violently for awhile, but without the force to bear them down. Our space will not permit us to more than glance at some of the incidents attendant on this singular crusade. The excitement that followed its inauguration in the large city of Cleveland was intense. It is thus described by Mrs. Sarah K. Bolton in her history of the Woman's Crusade, to which we have already referred:

HOW THE CRUSADERS WERE TREATED.

"The question was constantly asked: 'Will the women of a conservative city of one hundred and fifty thousand go upon the street as a praying-band?' The liquor-dealers said: 'Send committees of two or three and we will talk with them; but coming in a body to pray with us brands our business as disreputable.' The time came when the Master seemed to call for a mightier power to bear upon the liquor traffic, and a company of heroic women, many of them the wives of prominent clergymen, led by Mrs. W. A. Ingham, said: 'Here am I; the Lord's will be done.'

"On the third day of the street work, the whisky and beer interest seemed to have awakened to a full consciousness of the situation. Drinkers, dealers and roughs gathered in large numbers on the street to wait for the praying women. A mob, headed by an organization of brewers, rushed upon them, kicking them, striking them with their fists and hitting them with brickbats. The women were locked in a store away from the infuriated mob, who, on the arrival of a stronger body of police, were dispersed, cursing and yelling as they went. The next day, taking their lives in their hands, a larger company of women went out, and somewhat similar scenes were enacted. Meantime, public meetings, called in the churches, were so crowded that standing room could not be found. The clergy, as one man, came to the front. Business men left their stores and shops, ministers their studies, and a thousand manly men went out to defend the praying women. The military companies were ordered to be in readiness, resting on their arms; the police force was increased, and the liquor interest soon made to feel that the city was not under its control. The mob never again tried its power. For three months, with scarcely a day's exception, the praying-bands, sometimes with twenty in each, working in various parts of the city; sometimes with five hundred, quietly and silently, two by two, forming a procession over a quarter of a mile in length, followed by scores in carriages, who could not bear the long walks, went from saloon to saloon, holding services where the proprietors were willing, and in warehouses which were thrown open to them, or in vacant lots near by, when they were unwilling.

* * * Men took off their hats, and often wept as the long procession went by. Little children gathered close to the singers, and catching the words, sang them months afterwards in their dingy hovels. Haggard women bent their heads as they murmured with unutterable sadness, 'You've come too late to save my boy or my husband.' Many saloon-keepers gave up their business and never resumed it. Many who had lost all hope because of the appetite which bound them, heard from woman's lips the glad tidings of freedom in Christ, and accepted the liberty of the Gospel."

In many other places the crusaders met with violence from exasperated liquor-dealers and their brutish associates. A pail of cold water was thrown into the face of a woman in Clyde, Ohio, as she knelt praying in front of a saloon. Dirty water was thrown by pailfuls over the women at Norwalk. At Columbus, a saloon-keeper assaulted one of the praying-band, injuring her seriously. In Cincinnati, forty-three women were arrested by the authorities for praying in the street and lodged in jail. In Bellefontaine, a large liquor-dealer declared that if the praying-band visited him he would use powder and lead; but the women, undeterred by his threat, sang and prayed in front of his saloon every day for a week, in spite of the insults and noisy interferences of himself and customers. At the end of that time the man made his appearance at a mass-meeting and signed the pledge; and on the following Sunday attended church for the first time in five years.

DECLINE OF THE CRUSADING SPIRIT.

From Ohio the excitement soon spread to other Western States, and then passed east and south, until it was felt in nearly every State in the Union; but it did not gain force by extension. To the sober, second-thought of those who had, in singleness of heart, self-consecration and trust in God, thrown themselves into this work because they believed that they were drawn of the Spirit, came the perception of other, better and more orderly ways of accomplishing the good they sought. If God were, indeed, with them—if it was His Divine work of saving human souls upon which they had entered, He would lead them into the right ways, if they were but willing to walk therein. Of this there came to them a deep assurance; and in the great calm that fell after the rush and excitement and wild confusion of that first movement against the enemy, they heard the voice of God calling to them still. And, as they hearkened, waiting to be led, and willing to obey, light came, and they saw more clearly. Not by swift, impetuous impulse, but through organization and slow progression was the victory to be won.

In the language of Frances E. Willard, in her history of "The Woman's National Christian Temperance Union," to be found in the Centennial temperance volume: "The women who went forth by an impulse sudden, irresistible, divine, to pray in the saloons, became convinced, as weeks and months passed by, that theirs was to be no easily-won victory. The enemy was rich beyond their power to comprehend. He had upon his side the majesty of the law, the trickery of politics and the leagued strength of that almost invincible pair—appetite, avarice. He was persistent, too, as fate; determined to fight it out on that line to the last dollar of his enormous treasure-house and the last ounce of his power. But these women of the Crusade believed in God, and in themselves as among His appointed instruments to destroy the rum-power in America. They loved Christ's cause; they loved the native land that had been so mindful of them; they loved their sweet and sacred homes; and so it came about that, though they had gone forth only as skirmishers, they soon fell into line of battle; though they had ignorantly hoped to take the enemy by a sudden assault, they buckled on the armor for the long campaign. The woman's praying-bands, earnest, impetuous, inspired, became the woman's temperance unions, firm, patient, persevering. The praying-bands were without leadership, save that which inevitably results from 'the survival of the fittest;' the woman's unions are regularly officered in the usual way. They first wrought their grand pioneer work in sublime indifference to prescribed forms of procedure—'so say we all of us' being the spirit of 'motions' often made, seconded and carried by the chair, while the assembled women nodded their earnest acquiescence; the second are possessed of good, strong constitutions (with by-laws annexed), and follow the order of business with a dutiful regard to parliamentary usage. In the first, women who had never lifted up their voices in their own church prayer-meetings stood before thousands and 'spoke as they were moved;' in the second, these same women with added experience, and a host of others who have since enlisted, impress the public thought and conscience by utterances carefully considered. The praying-bands, hoping for immediate victory, pressed their members into incessant service; the woman's unions, aware that the battle is to be a long one, ask only for such help as can be given consistently with other duties."

As the result of this intelligent effort at effective organization by the women who inaugurated and were prominent in the "Crusade," we have "The Woman's National Christian Temperance Union," with its auxiliary and local unions in nearly every State; one of the most efficient agencies in the practical work of temperance reform which the country has yet seen.

CHAPTER XII.

THE WOMAN'S NATIONAL CHRISTIAN TEMPERANCE UNION.

DURING the summer of 1874, when the reaction which had checked the "Crusade" was recognized as something permanent by the more thoughtful and observant of the women who had been engaged in it, they paused for deliberation, and took counsel together. Great victories had been won in the brief season during which they were masters of the field; and now that the enemy had rallied his forces, and intrenched himself behind law, public opinion, politics and the State, should they weakly give up the contest? Not so. They had discovered wherein the weakness, as well as the strength, of their enemy lay, and had come into a new perception of their own powers and resources.

ORGANIZATION.

The first step taken was to call conventions in the various States where the Crusade had been active. These were attended by delegates chosen by the local praying-bands. The result was the organization, in some of the States, of what were known as "Temperance Leagues." Afterwards the word "Unions" was substituted for Leagues. Having organized by States, the next thing was to have a National Union. In August of that year, the first National Sunday-School Assembly was held at Chautauqua Lake, near Buffalo, New York. Many of the most earnest workers in the temperance Crusade, from different parts of the United States, and from the various denominations of Christians, were present, and the conviction was general that steps should at once be taken towards forming a National League, in order to make permanent the work that had already been done. After much deliberation, a committee of organization was appointed, consisting of a woman from each State. This committee issued a circular letter, asking the various Woman's Temperance Leagues to hold meetings, for the purpose of electing one woman from each Congressional district as a delegate to a National Convention, to be held in November, at Cleveland, Ohio. A single paragraph from this circular will show the spirit that animated the call.

"It is hardly necessary to remind those who have worked so nobly in the grand temperance uprising that in union and organization are its success and permanence, and the consequent redemption of this land from the curse of intemperance. In the name of our Master—in behalf of the thousands of women who suffer from this terrible evil, we call upon all to unite in an earnest, continued effort to hold the ground already won, and move onward together to a complete victory over the foes we fight."

Delegates representing sixteen States were present at the convention, which held its first session in Cleveland, commencing on the 18th of November, 1874, and lasting for three days. Prominent among its members were active leaders of the Crusade, but, besides these, says Miss Willard, "there were present many thoughtful and gifted women, whose hearts had been stirred by the great movement, though until now they had lacked the opportunity to identify themselves with it. Mrs. Jennie F. Willing presided over the convention, which was one of the most earnest and enthusiastic ever held. A constitution was adopted, also a plan of organization intended to reach every hamlet, town and city in the land. There was a declaration of principles, of which Christianity alone could have furnished the animus. An appeal to the women of our country was provided for; another to the girls of America; a third to lands beyond the sea; a memorial to Congress was ordered, and a deputation to carry it appointed; a National temperance paper, to be edited and published by women, was agreed upon, also a financial plan, asking for a cent a week from members; and last, not least, was appointed a special committee on temperance work among the children. Four large mass-meetings were held during the convention, all of them addressed by women. Mrs. Annie Wittenmyer, of Philadelphia, was elected president; Miss Frances E. Willard, of Chicago, corresponding secretary; Mrs. Mary C. Johnson, of Brooklyn, recording secretary; Mrs. Mary A. Ingham, of Cleveland, treasurer, with one vice-president from each State represented in the convention."

The spirit of this assembly of workers is shown in the closing resolution, which it adopted unanimously:

> "*Resolved*, That, recognizing the fact that our cause is, and is to be, combated by mighty, determined and relentless forces, we will, trusting in Him who is the Prince of Peace, meet argument with argument, misjudgment with patience, denunciation with kindness, and all our difficulties and dangers with prayer."

FIRST YEAR'S WORK.

During the first year six State organizations were added to the number represented in the beginning, including scores of local unions. A monthly paper was established; a deputation of women sent to Congress with a memorial, to which hundreds of thousands of signatures had been obtained, asking for inquiry and legislation in regard to the liquor traffic; a manual of "Hints and Helps," concerning methods of temperance work, prepared and issued; and other agencies of reform, and for the extermination of the liquor traffic, set in motion.

The reports from State Unions, made to the first annual meeting, held in Cincinnati, November, 1875, were, in most cases, highly encouraging. In Ohio, a large number of local unions were formed, nearly two hundred friendly inns established, while reading-rooms, juvenile societies and young people's leagues were reported as multiplying all over the State. Indiana showed effective work in the same direction; so did Illinois. In both of these States many local unions, reform clubs and juvenile organizations came into existence, while the work of temperance agitation was carried on with untiring vigor. Iowa reported fifty local unions, eleven juvenile societies, seven reform clubs and six coffee-houses and reading-rooms. But, how better can we sum up the results of this year's work, and how better give a clear idea of the new forces which were coming into the field under the leadership of women, than by giving an extract from the first annual report of the corresponding secretary, Miss Frances E. Willard:

"Briefly to recapitulate, bringing out salient features, Maine has given, since the Crusade, the idea of the temperance camp-meeting, which, though not original with us, has been rendered effective largely through the efforts of our own workers. Connecticut influences elections, has availed itself of petitions and given us the best form on record. New York has kept alive the visitation of saloons, and proved, what may we never forget, that this is always practicable, if conducted wisely. In the relief and rescue branches of our work, the Empire State is perhaps without a rival. The women of

Pennsylvania have bearded the gubernatorial lion in his den, and the Hartranft veto had the added sin of women's prayers and tears denied. Maryland and the District of Columbia prove that the North must look to her laurels when the South is free to enter on our work. As for Ohio, as Daniel Webster said of the old Bay State, 'There she stands; look at her!'—foremost among leaders in the new Crusade. Michigan is working bravely amid discouragements. Illinois has given us the most promising phase of our juvenile work, and leads off in reform clubs. Our best organized States are Ohio, Indiana, New York, Pennsylvania and Iowa. By reason of their multiplied conventions of State, district and county, their numerous auxilaries, their petitions and their juvenile work, Ohio and Indiana bear off the palm, and stand as the banner States of our Union up to this time, each of them having as many as two hundred and fifty auxiliaries.

"Our review develops the fact that of the forty-seven States and Territories forming the United States, twenty-two States have formed temperance unions auxiliary to the Woman's National Union. Of the twenty-five not yet organized, twelve are Southern States and eight are Territories; while of the remaining five, three are about to organize State unions, and have already flourishing local unions. So, that, without exaggeration, we may say we have fairly entered into the land to possess it. To bring about this vast result of organization, and to maintain it, there have been held (not to mention conventions of districts and counties, the name of which is legion,) forty-five State conventions of women, almost all within the last year.

"The number of written communications sent out during the year from our Western office to women in every State in the Union, is nearly five thousand. This is exclusive of 'documents,' which have gone by the bushel from the Eastern and Western offices, and also of the incessant correspondence of our president. Either president or secretary has spoken in nearly every State in which our organization exists. During the summer months, conventions, camp-meetings and local auxiliaries in large numbers have been addressed by officers of our National and State Unions in all of the Eastern and Middle and in many of the Western States. Noteworthy in our history for the year, is the monster petition circulated in nearly every State, presented to Congress on our behalf by Senator Morton, of Indiana, and defended in an eloquent speech before the Finance Committee by our president."

THE SECOND YEAR'S WORK.

The second annual meeting of the "Woman's National Christian Temperance Union" was held in Newark, N. J., in October, 1876. From the reports made to this meeting, we take the following interesting statements, showing how actively the work, for which this great National Association was organized, has been prosecuted.

Twenty-two State unions were represented at this meeting, and local unions were reported as having been formed for the first time in Tennessee, Louisiana and Arkansas, preparatory to State organizations. An International Temperance Convention of women had been held in the Academy of Music, Philadelphia, from which resulted an International Woman's Temperance Union. A summary of the work of the year says:

"In almost every organized State, the request of our National Committee that ministerial, medical and educational associations be asked to declare their position in relation to temperance reform has been complied with. In every instance, the ladies have been courteously received, and in no case has the declaration of opinion been adverse, and in many, most hopeful to our cause. The letter of Mrs. Wittenmyer to the International Medical Convention recently held in Philadelphia, secured the important declaration against alcohol made by that body.

"In February, our president, accompanied by Mrs. Mary R. Denman, President of New Jersey W. T. U., made a trip to Kentucky, Tennessee and Louisiana, in the endeavor to enlist our Southern sisters in the temperance work. Large meetings were addressed and several local unions organized.

"In the month of May thirty-six temperance meetings were held in the State of Ohio, by the corresponding secretary, who has also made a trip through Michigan, and spoken in all the Eastern, Middle and several of the Western States since the last meeting.

"Our recording secretary, Mrs. Mary C. Johnson, has visited Great Britian, by invitation of Christian women there, for the purpose of introducing our Gospel work. Going in the spirit of the Crusade, Mrs. Johnson's labors have awakened an earnest spirit of inquiry and activity among the thoughtful and comparatively leisure class. During her six months' absence in England and Ireland, she addressed one hundred and twenty-one audiences and conducted forty prayer-meetings.

"'Mother Stewart,' of Ohio, has also visited England and Scotland this year, under the auspices of the Good Templars, and much good has resulted from her labors.

"Our union has circulated the petition to Congress for a Commission of Inquiry into the costs and results of the liquor traffic in America, and to the Centennial Commissioners praying them not to allow the sale of intoxicants on the Exposition grounds. The desired Commission of Inquiry has been ordered by the Senate in response to the wish of the united temperance societies of the land, but the subject did not come before the House at the last session.

"Our paper has constantly increased in its hold upon the local unions, whose devotion to its interests augurs well for its future success.

"The number of documents scattered among our auxiliaries cannot be accurately stated, but is not less than twelve or fifteen thousand, and the correspondence of the officers by letter and postal-card, will not fall short of the same estimate. To correct misapprehensions, it should, perhaps, be stated that no officer of the National Union has received a dollar for services or traveling expenses during the year."

A WORKING ORGANIZATION.

To meet annually in convention and pass resolutions and make promises is one thing; to do practical and effective work all through the year is quite another. And it is just here that this new temperance organization exhibits its power. The women whom it represents are very much in earnest and mean work. What they resolve to do, if clearly seen to be in the right direction, will hardly fail for lack of effort. In their plan of work, one branch particularly embraces the children. If the rising generation can not only be pledged to abstinence, but so carefully instructed in regard to the sin and evil of intemperance, and their duty, when they become men and women, to make war upon the liquor traffic, and to discountenance all form of social drinking, then an immense gain will be had for the cause in the next generation, when the boys and girls of to-day will hold the ballots, make the laws, give direction to public sentiment and determine the usages of society.

LOOKING AFTER THE CHILDREN.

To what extent, then, are the State and local unions looking after the children? Writing, as we now are, before the third annual meeting of the National Union, and, therefore, without a general report of the year's work before us, we are unable to give a statement in full of the important temperance work which has been done with and for the rising generation. But, from official and other reliable sources of information, we are in possession of facts of a most gratifying character. In the State of Minnesota, as the result of woman's efforts, they have had for several years a "Sunday-School Temperance League," and their last annual report gives seventeen thousand as the number of children already "pledged to abstain from all intoxicants as a beverage." Says their report for 1877, "We have carried the work into sixty-one new schools, held sixty-three anniversary meetings and temperance concerts, instigated about one thousand addresses in the Sunday-schools, secured six thousand six hundred and seventy-four signers to our pledges, and one thousand and fifteen to our constitution."

In most of the larger towns throughout the United States where active local unions exist, juvenile unions, bands of hope or temperance associations by some other name, have been formed among the children. These have, in many cases, a large membership; often as high as from five to six hundred. In Rockford, Ill., the juvenile union numbers over eight hundred boys and as many girls. The pledge taken by these children includes, in some localities, tobacco and profanity as well as intoxicants.

THE WORK OF REFORM AND RESCUE.

In the work of reform and rescue, the State and local unions are very active, especially in the larger towns and cities. In the smaller towns, religious temperance meetings are held weekly, and in the larger cities, daily, and sometimes twice a day. Chicago has as many as eighteen meetings every week. In Chapters XIX. and XX. of the first part of this volume, we have described at length, and from personal observation, the way in which these temperance prayer-meetings are generally conducted, and the means used for lifting up and saving the poor drunkard.

What are known as "Reform Clubs," have grown out of the efforts made of these praying women, to hold in safety the men whom they have been able to rescue. These clubs are numerous in New England and the Western States, and have a large membership, which is composed exclusively of reformed men. The common platform upon which they all stand is: 1. Total abstinence. 2. Reliance upon God's help in all things. 3. Missionary work to induce others to sign the pledge. In Newark, N. J., there is a club with a membership of over six hundred reformed men, nearly all of whom have been rescued in the past three years, through the efforts of the Woman's Christian Temperance Union of that city.

In an interview with Mrs. Wittenmyer, President of the National Union, who had received reports of the third year's work from the various unions, we learned that, after deducting from the returns all who were known to have broken the pledge, ten thousand remained as the number reported to have been saved during the year, and who were still standing in the strength which God had given them. The larger part of these rescued men had united themselves with the church, and were earnestly endeavoring to lead Christian lives.

KEEPING ALIVE A SENTIMENT ADVERSE TO THE LIQUOR TRAFFIC.

Another and most important branch of the work of the "Woman's Christian Temperance Union," is that of arousing, keeping alive and intensifying a sentiment adverse to the liquor traffic. So long as the State and National Governments give the sanction of law to this traffic, they find their efforts to save the fallen, utterly unavailing in far too many instances. In an appeal made by the women of the State Union to the voters of Massachusetts, under date of August 15th, 1877, the curse of this traffic is exhibited in words of solemn earnestness. The document is strong and convincing, yet temperate and respectful. We copy it entire as presenting arguments and considerations which every humane and

Christian voter in the land should lay deeply to heart:

"The Woman's Christian Temperance Union comes to you with a solemn and earnest appeal.

"Our mission is the redemption of the Commonwealth from the curse of intemperance. During the past year we have labored incessantly for this end, and have expended nearly twenty thousand dollars in efforts to rescue the perishing, and to educate public sentiment in favor of total abstinence.

"In this work we have met numerous obstacles—the apathy of the people, the inherited and depraved appetites of drunkards, and the perilous social customs of the day, which are indorsed by the practice of many otherwise excellent people. Worse than all these combined is the influence of the licensed dram-shop. We can arouse the indifferent to action; we can enkindle in the drunkard aspirations for a better life than that of debauchery; we hope, in time, by constant agitation, to change the social customs of the day. But against the influence of the licensed dram-shop we are powerless. We have no ability to cope with this most formidable enemy of virtue, prosperity and good order.

"A long and bitter experience compels us to say that the most untiring efforts to reclaim the drunkard have, in many instances, proved unavailing, because his demoralized will has been powerless to resist the temptations placed in his path by the sanction of the State.

"Worse, if possible, even than this—the licensed dram-shop is instrumental in creating a new generation of drunkards. For thither resort our young men, the future hope of the country, who speedily fall before the seductions of the place, their habits of sobriety are subverted, their moral sense is blunted, their will palsied, and they drift rapidly into the appalling condition of habitual drunkenness. The licensed dram-shops are recruiting offices, where another army of drunkards is enlisted, to fill the ranks depleted by dishonored deaths—and the great Commonwealth extends over them the ægis of its protection, indorsing them by the sanction of law. The people of Massachusetts drink annually twenty-five million dollars' worth of intoxicating liquors. *Only God can furnish the statistics of sorrow, poverty, disease, vice and crime, begotten by this fearful consumption of strong drink.*

"Under these discouraging circumstances, men of Massachusetts, we appeal to you! The licensed dram-shop is the creature of political action. We are wholly destitute of political power, by which it must be overthrown. Anguished by the peril of fathers and brothers, husbands and sons, we appeal to you to make good the oft-repeated assertion that the men of the State represent and protect the women of the State at the ballot-box. We beseech you to make earnest efforts to secure the repeal of the license law at the next election, and the enactment of a law prohibiting the sale of intoxicating liquors as a beverage.

"We are sure we speak the sentiment of the Christian people of this State, and of all who stand for morality, thrift, virtue and good order, when we say that the great State of Massachusetts should not take sides with the drunkard-maker against his victim. If either is to be protected by law, it should be the drunkard, since he is the weaker, rather than the rumseller, who persistently blocks the pathway of reform.

"We know that we utter the voice of the majority of the women of the State when we plead the cause of prohibition—and the women of Massachusetts outnumbers its men by more than sixty thousand. It is women who are the greatest sufferers from the licensed dram-shops of the community—and we pray you, therefore, voters of Massachusetts, to take such action that the law which protects these drinking shops may be blotted from the statute book at the next election."

This appeal from the Christian women of Massachusetts is signed by Mrs. Mary A. Livermore, President, and Mrs. L. B. Barrett, Secretary of the State branch of the Woman's National Temperance Union, and shows the animating spirit of that body. No one can read it without a new impression of the wickedness of a traffic that curses everything it touches.

But not alone in Massachusetts are the women of

the "Union" using their efforts to shape public opinion and influence the ballot. In all the States where unions exist, this part of the work is steadily prosecuted; and it cannot be long ere its good results will become manifest at the polls in a steadily increasing anti-license vote, and, ultimately in the ranging of State after State with Maine, Vermont and New Hampshire on the side of prohibition.

INFLUENCE ON THE MEDICAL PROFESSION.

In still another direction important gains have been realized. But for the efforts of the Woman's National and State Temperance Unions we should scarcely have had the declaration of the International Medical Congress of 1876, adverse to the use of alcohol as food or medicine. Early in their work, the women of the "Union," seeing how largely the medical prescription of alcohol was hurting the cause of temperance, and being in possession of the latest results of chemical and physiological investigation in regard to its specific action on the body, sent delegations to various State medical associations at their annual meetings, urging them to pass resolutions defining its true status as a food or a medicine and discouraging its use in the profession. With most of these medical associations they found a respectful hearing; and their presentation of the matter had the effect of drawing to the subject the attention of a large number of medical men who had not, from old prejudices, or in consequence of their absorption in professional duties, given careful attention to the later results of scientific investigation. As a consequence, many physicians who had been in the habit of ordering alcoholic stimulants for weak or convalescent patients, gave up the practice entirely; while those who still resorted to their use, deemed it safest to be more guarded in their administration than heretofore.

ACTION OF THE INTERNATIONAL MEDICAL CONGRESS.

But the crowning result of this effort to induce the medical profession to limit or abandon the prescription of alcohol, came when the International Congress, one of the largest and ablest medical bodies ever convened, made, through its "Section on Medicine," the brief, but clear and unequivocal declaration already given in a previous chapter, and at once and forever laid upon alcohol the ban of the profession.

Official communications were addressed to this body by the National Temperance Society, through its president, Hon. Wm. E. Dodge, by the Woman's Christian Temperance Union, through its president, Mrs. Annie Wittenmyer, and by the New York Friends' Temperance Union, asking from it a declaration as to the true character of alcohol and its value in medicine.

The following is the full text of the memorial of the Woman's Christian Temperance Union:

"*To the Chairman and Members of the International Medical Congress:*

"HONORED SIRS:—I take the liberty, as a representative of the Woman's National Christian Temperance Union of the United States, to call your attention to the relation of the medical use of alcohol to the prevalence of that fearful scourge, *intemperance.*

"The distinguished Dr. Mussey said, many years ago: 'So long as alcohol retains a place among sick patients, so long there will be drunkards.'

"Dr. Rush wrote strongly against its use as early as 1790. And at one time the College of Physicians at Philadelphia memorialized Congress in favor of restraining the use of distilled liquors, because, as they claimed, they were 'destructive of life, health and the faculties of the mind.'

"'A Medical Declaration,' published in London, December, 1872, asserts that 'it is believed that the inconsiderate prescription of alcoholic liquids by medical men for their patients has given rise, in many instances, to the formation of intemperate habits.' This manifesto was signed by over two hundred and fifty of the leading medical men of the United Kingdom. When the nature and effects of alcohol were little known, it was thought to be invaluable as a medicine. But in the light of recent scientific investigations, its claims have been challenged and its value denied.

"We are aware that the question of the medical

use of alcohol has not been fully decided, and that there is a difference of opinion among the ablest medical writers. But we notice that as the discussion and investigation goes on, and the new facts are brought out, its value as a remedial agent is depreciated.

"A great many claims have been brought forward in its favor, but one by one they have gone down under the severe scrutiny of scientific research, until only a few points are left in doubt. In view of this, and the *startling fact* that tens of thousands die annually from its baneful effects, we earnestly urge you to give the subject a careful examination.

"You have made the study of the physical nature of man your life-work, and you are the trusted advisers of the people in all matters pertaining to the treatment of diseases and the preservation of life and health.

"You are, therefore, in a position to instruct and warn the masses in regard to its indiscriminate use, either as a medicine or a beverage.

"We feel sure that, true to your professional honor, and the grave responsibilities of your distinguished position, you will search out and give us the facts, whatever they may be.

"If you should appoint a standing committee from your own number, of practical scientific men, who would give time and thought to this question, it would be very gratifying to the *one hundred*

A VICTIM OF THE DRINKING CLUB.

thousand women I represent, and most acceptable to the general public.

"I am, with high considerations of respect,

"Your obed't servant,

"ANNIE WITTENMYER,

"*Pres't W. Nat. Chris. Temp. Union.*

"*Philadelphia, Sept. 6th,* 1876."

How was this memorial received? Scarcely had it been presented ere a member moved that it be laid on the table without reading; but ere the vote could be taken the voice of another member rose clear and strong in the question whether that body could afford to treat a hundred thousand American women with such a discourtesy! And the motion to lay on the table was lost.

A vote to refer to the "Section on Medicine" was largely carried; and to that section the petitioners took their case, and were not only accorded a gracious and respectful hearing, but, after a full discussion of the subject, a declaration against the use of alcohol, as a substance both hurtful and dangerous—possessing no food value whatever, and as a medicine, being exceedingly limited in its range. All the points in reply were passed upon unanimously by the section to which the matter was referred, and afterwards by the Congress in full session, with but a single dissenting vote, and the result officially communicated to the president of the Woman's Christian Temperance Union. An official notification of the action of the Congress was also sent to Hon. Wm. E. Dodge, president of the National Temperance Society.

Other aspects of the work of this young and vigorous organization might be given; but enough has been presented to show that its agency in temperance reform is already far-reaching and powerful; and to give assurance that if the spirit which has influenced and directed its counsels so wisely from the beginning, can be maintained, it will achieve still greater and more important victories for the cause of temperance.

CHAPTER XIII.

REFORM CLUBS.

THESE differ in some aspects from most of the associations which, prior to their organization, had for their object the reformation of men who had fallen into habits of drunkenness. The distinguishing characteristics of the reform club is its religious spirit, its dependence upon God and its reliance upon prayer.

The first movement in this direction was made in Gardiner, Maine, in January, 1872, by Mr. I. K. Osgood. He says of himself that in fifteen years he had run down from a moderate and fashionable drinker of wine, to a constant and immoderate drinker of the vilest spirits; and from the condition of a respectable business man to one of misery and destitution. Coming back to his wretched home late one night, he saw through the window his poor wife sitting lonely and sorrowful, waiting for his return. The sight touched his heart and caused him to reflect, and then to resolve, that God being his helper he would never drink again. That resolution he found himself able, by God's help, to keep. A few months later he began the work of trying to reform others. His first effort was with a lawyer, an old friend, who was as much reduced by drink as he had been. After much entreaty, this man consented to break off drinking and sign the pledge. Mr. Osgood then drew up the following call for a meeting which both signed: "REFORMERS' MEETING.—There will be a meeting of reformed drinkers at City Hall, Gardiner, on Friday evening, January 19th, at seven o'clock. A cordial invitation is extended to all occasional drinkers, constant drinkers, hard drinkers and young men who are tempted to drink. Come and hear what rum has done for us."

A crowd came to the City Hall. The two men addressed the meeting with great earnestness, and then offered the pledge, which was signed by eight of their old drinking companions. These organized themselves into a reform club, which soon reached a hundred members, all of whom had been men of intemperate habits. The movement soon attracted attention in other places, especially among drinking men, and clubs multiplied rapidly throughout the State. In a few months, the aggregate membership reached nearly twenty thousand. In June of the following year, Mr. Osgood began his work in Massachusetts, under the auspices of the Massachusetts Temperance Alliance, organizing about forty clubs, one of which, in Haverill, numbered over three thousand members. In New Hampshire and Vermont, many clubs were organized by Mr. Osgood and some of his converts.

DR. HENRY A. REYNOLDS.

Another effective worker in the field is Dr. Henry A. Reynolds, of Bangor, Maine, where he was born in 1839. In 1863, he graduated from the Medical College of Harvard University, and was assistant surgeon in the First Maine Regiment, heavy artillery, during two years of the war, receiving an honorable discharge. He then entered upon the practice of medicine in his native city, and continued therein until 1874. But he had inherited a taste for strong drink, through the indulgence of which he became its abject slave. After many efforts at reform which proved of no avail, he resolved to look to Almighty God, and ask for strength to overcome his dreadful appetite. About this time there was, in the city of Bangor, a band of Christian women who met frequently to pray for the salvation of the intemperate. At one of their meetings, the doctor presented himself—it was two days after he had knelt alone in his office and prayed to God for help—and publicly signed the pledge.

Sympathy for those who were in the dreadful slough from which he had been lifted, soon began stirring in his heart, and he sought, by various methods, to influence and save them. After working for several months, with only partial success, it became evident, that for sure and permanent work, there must be organization, and he conceived the plan of a reform club made up exclusively of those who had been drinking men; believing, as he did, that there must exist between two men who had once been intemperate, a sympathy which could not exist between a man who has; and one who has never, drank to excess. As soon as this matter became clear to him, Dr. Reynolds, by notice in a daily paper, invited the drinking men of the city to meet him at a certain place. Eleven men responded to the call, and the Bangor Reform Club, the first of its kind, was organized, September 10th, 1874, with Dr. Henry A. Reynolds as president. The motto of the new organization was, "Dare to do Right." Filled with the true missionary spirit, this little band held other meetings, and did their utmost to bring in new members, and so successful were their efforts, that in a few weeks their membership swelled to hundreds, and the whole city was in a state of excitement over the new and strange work which had been inaugurated.

From Bangor, the excitement soon spread through the State. Dr. Reynolds, believing that God had called him to the work of saving men from intemperance and leading them to Christ, gave up his profession and threw himself into the work of preaching temperance and organizing reform clubs. Within a year forty-five thousand reformed men were gathered into clubs in the State of Maine. In August, 1875, at a meeting of the National Christian Temperance Camp-Meeting Association, held at Old Orchard, Maine, where temperance workers from all parts of the country had congregated, the president of the Woman's Christian Temperance Union of Salem, Massachusetts, learned of the great work of reform progressing in Maine under the leadership of Dr. Reynolds, and invited him to introduce his work in Massachusetts by holding a series of meetings in Salem during the month of September. So the work began in the Old Bay State, and within a year, forty thousand men of that Commonwealth, who had been habitual drinkers, were organized into reform clubs.

FORMATION OF CLUBS.

The method pursued by Dr. Reynolds in the formation of these clubs is very simple. There is a constitution with by-laws, to which the following pledge is prefixed: "Having seen and felt the evils of intemperance, therefore, Resolved, That we, the undersigned, for our own good and the good of the world in which we live, do hereby promise and engage, with the help of Almighty God, to abstain from buying, selling or using alcoholic or malt beverages, wine and cider included." Article III. of the constitution gives the qualification for membership: "All male persons of the age of eighteen or upwards, who have been in the habit of using intoxicating liquor to a greater or less extent, are eligible to membership in this club." After organizing a club of persons who have been addicted to drink, Dr. Reynolds appeals to the Christian women of the locality to throw around them the shield of their care and sympathy, and urges upon the people at large the necessity of upholding and encouraging them in every possible way.

The meetings of the clubs are held at least once during the week, in the evenings; and on Sunday afternoons or evenings, the clubs, with the Woman's Christian Temperance Unions, hold public religious temperance meetings, which are often crowded to overflowing. The order of exercises at these public meetings consist of prayer, reading of Scripture and brief addresses by reformed men, interspersed with the singing of such hymns as "Rock of Ages," "Hold the Fort," "I Need Thee Every Hour," etc. Brief addresses are the rule, and a hymn is usually sung between each address.

The badge worn by members of these reformed clubs is a red ribbon. Their motto is "Dare to do Right."

One of the first fruits of the establishment of a reform club in any locality, is an increase in church attendance, and a decrease in the tax rate. In many towns where they exist, liquor-selling has become unprofitable, and liquor-drinking a custom that hurts a man's social standing.

From the East, Dr. Reynolds extended his labors into the West, where his work has been chiefly confined to the State of Michigan. In a letter to the *Union*, the organ of the Woman's Christian Temperance Union, under date of July, 1877, the aspect and results of Dr. Reynolds's work in that State are thus referred to by a correspondent from Evanston: "His plan is to take a State and settle down in it 'to stay' until it capitulates to the red-ribbon pledge. None but men over eighteen years of age are allowed to sign this pledge. Eighty thousand men in Michigan, to-day, wear the ribbon, which is a token of their signature—all of them have been drinking men. 'None others need apply' as members of Dr. Reynolds's Reform Clubs. His method is to speak in a general way to the public on the evening of his arrival—his meetings being held in a hall and thoroughly announced. The next afternoon, the doctor addresses women, chiefly from the medical point of view. If they have not a W. T. U. he organizes one. The second night he talks to the public generally again, and organizes his club, then goes on his way, and leaves the town rejoicing. The doctor is thoroughly business-like and methodical. There is no doubt about his securing, in every State he visits, the same results as in Michigan, for his ability is marked, his experience growing, his sincerity complete and all his work is 'begun, continued and ended' in a firm reliance upon God."

To give an idea of the excitement created by the presence of Dr. Reynolds in any community, and of the results of his efforts to reclaim intemperate men, we copy the following brief reference to his work in the spring of 1877:

"It is impossible to give figures, for there are additions every day of hundreds in the State, and the climax of enthusiasm is by no means reached in any town while Dr. Reynolds is there.

"In Jackson, Sabbath evening, February 11th, two months after the organization of the club, Union Hall was so packed that the galleries settled and were cleared, and hundreds could not gain admittance.

"As the result of ten days' work in Saginaw Valley—at the three cities—(Bay City, Saginaw City and East Saginaw), the clubs number about three thousand men.

"From there, Dr. Reynolds went to Lansing, our capital, and at the first signing, two hundred and forty-five joined the club, which is far up in the hundreds now.

"The last and greatest victory is Detroit. Slow, critical, conservative, staid, not-any-shams-for-me Detroit.

"Friday and Saturday nights there were crowded houses. Sabbath afternoon, two thousand five hundred *men* together, and a club of three hundred and forty-five formed. Sabbath evening, no room could hold the people, and the club reached nearly nine hundred. It is safe to say to-day that a thousand men in the city of Detroit are wearing the red ribbon.

"Dr. Reynolds has done another grand work, and that is in bringing up the W. C. T. Unions. Everywhere this follows, churches are packed with women. Dr. Reynolds tells them how they can help the men and their families, and they fall into line by the hundreds. Three hundred have enlisted in Bay City, four hundred in Lansing, two hundred in East Saginaw, and so on, all over the State."

The establishment of reform clubs has been more general in New England and the Western States than in other parts of the country, though their organization in some of the Middle States has been attended with marked success. Vermont has a large number of clubs, the membership ranging from one hundred to fifteen hundred.

FRANCIS MURPHY.

The work of Francis Murphy, which has been attended with such remarkable fervors of excitement in nearly every community where he has labored, is not so definite in its purpose, nor so closely organized, nor so permanent in its results as that of Dr. Reynolds. He draws vast assemblies, and obtains large numbers of signers to his pledge, which reads:

"With malice towards none and charity for all, I, the undersigned, do pledge my word and honor, God helping me, to abstain from all intoxicating liquors as a beverage, and that I will, by all honorable means, encourage others to abstain."

An Irishman by birth, and full of the warm impulse and quick enthusiasm of his people, he has thrown himself into the work of temperance reform with an earnestness that commands a hearing, and with an ardor of appeal and solicitation that is, for the time, almost irresistible.

In the fall of 1869, Francis Murphy found himself in the cell of a prison in the city of Portland, Maine, to which he had been committed for drunkenness. He had been a liquor-seller, commencing the work as a sober man with a good character, and ending it in ruin to himself and family, and with the curse of the drunkard's appetite upon him. A Christian gentleman, Captain Cyrus Sturdevant, had obtained permission of the authorities to visit the jail and talk and pray with the prisoners. This brought him into personal contact with Mr. Murphy, who was not only deeply humiliated at the disgrace into which his intemperate life had brought him, but almost in despair. He tells the story of this part of his life with a moving eloquence. Capt. Sturdevant, after some solicitation, induced him to leave his cell one Sunday morning and attend religious services with the prisoners. He was in a state of mind to be deeply impressed by these services, and the result was a solemn resolution to walk, with God's help, in a new and better way. While yet a prisoner, he began his work of trying to save men from the curse of drink, and to lead them to enter upon a religious life; and his influence with his fellow-prisoners was very marked and for good. On leaving the jail, he began at once his efforts to rescue others from the slavery from which he had escaped. His first appearance as a lecturer was in the city of Portland. The effort was well received by the audience, and at its close he found himself an object of special interest. From this time, he gave himself almost wholly to the cause of temperance. After working for a time in Portland, and assisting in the organization of a reform club, he extended his efforts to other parts of the State of Maine, and afterwards to New Hampshire and the adjoining States, in which he labored for nearly three years with marked and often extraordinary success. From New England, Mr. Murphy went, on invitation, to the West, and was very active there, especially in Iowa and Illinois, in which States he aroused the people, and was instrumental in the organization of large numbers of local societies and reform clubs.

In the winter of 1876-7, his work in Pittsburgh was attended with remarkable results; over sixty thousand signatures were obtained to his pledge, and over five hundred saloons in Allegheny and neighboring counties closed their doors for want of patronage. The succeeding spring and summer Mr. Murphy spent in Philadelphia, where the excitement was almost as great as it had been in Pittsburgh. But, as in the last-named city, too large a portion of the harvest which had been reaped was left to perish on the ground for lack of the means, or the will, to gather and garner it. The real substantial and enduring work here has been that of the Woman's Christian Temperance Union; which not only held its meetings daily during the exciting time of the Murphy meetings, but has held them daily ever since, keeping, all the while, hand and heart upon the men who are trying in earnest to reform, and helping, encouraging and protecting them by all the means in their power.

Mr. Murphy continues to work in various parts of the country, attracting large audiences wherever he appears, and leading thousands to sign his pledge. He has done and is still doing good service in the cause to which he is so earnestly devoting himself.

CHAPTER XIV.

GOSPEL TEMPERANCE.

AS we have seen in the chapters on the "Crusade," the "Woman's Christian Temperance Union," and the "Reform Clubs," this new temperance movement, which has attained in the last few years such large dimensions, has in it many of the features of a religious revival. On this account, and to distinguish it from all preceding efforts to break down the liquor traffic and save the drunkard, it has been called a Gospel temperance movement. Its chief reliance with many has been on prayer and faith, as agencies by which the mighty power of God could be so determined as not only to save the drunkard from the curse of his debasing appetite, but to so move and act upon the liquor-seller as to lead him to abandon his accursed traffic.

THE VALUE OF PRAYER AND FAITH ALONE.

At the commencement of this movement, which took the form of what is known as the "Woman's Crusade," the power of prayer seemed for awhile to be an almost irresistible force. Thousands and tens of thousands of men were, as they felt assured in their hearts, freed in an instant of time from an appetite which had been growing and strengthening for years, until it held complete mastery over them; and this in answer to the prayer of faith. And hundreds of saloon and tavern-keepers abandoned their evil work, because, as was believed, God, in answer to the prayers of pious men and women, had turned upon them the influences of His Holy Spirit, and constrained them to this abandonment.

For awhile this power of prayer was regarded as the force that was to break down the liquor traffic, and rescue the people from the curse of appetite. If prayer were persistent enough, and faith strong enough, God would come to the rescue, overthrow the enemy, and redeem and save the wretched victims he was holding in such cruel bondage. But, as time moved on, and the enemy, whose ranks were at first thrown into confusion, rallied his forces and held himself secure against renewed attack, there came a doubt in the minds of many as to the value of prayer and faith as the sole agency by which the rule of the demon of intemperance was to be overthrown; and the same doubt came as to the power of prayer and faith alone to work the removal of an appetite for drink, when it was found by sad experience that of the thousands of men who signed the pledge under religious excitement, and made public declaration that, through faith in Christ, they had been healed of their infirmity, only a few were able to stand in the hour of temptation; and these stood fast because they rested in no vain security. They knew, from an inner conviction, that appetite had not been destroyed; and that, in some unguarded moment, it would spring upon and endeavor to enslave them again. But, with God's help, they had resolved to hold it in check. Humbly they looked to Him for strength—meantime watching, as well as praying—to fight and overcome when their hour of trial and darkness came. So they stood ever on guard; and God gave them the strength they asked for, and victory after victory, until their enemy was under their feet; not dead, but held there by the power which is given to every one who will use it against the enemies of his soul.

PRAYER SUPPLEMENTED BY ORGANIZED WORK.

Not so much dependence on prayer and faith now as on organized work in the natural plane of means and forces. This came as an orderly sequence, and gave to the cause of Gospel temperance a surer foundation to rest upon, and a larger promise of success. There was no turning away from God; no weakness of faith in His Divine power and readiness to save; but clearer light as to His ways with man, and as to how He is able to save, to the uttermost, all who come unto Him. The instances going to show that men were not cured of the appetite for strong drink in a moment of time by prayer and faith, were too many and too sorrowful not to force this conviction upon the mind of every thoughtful and observant Christian man and woman. And, so, even while many sincere and self-devoted workers in this cause still hold to the view that God can, and will, if the faith be strong enough, change a man in an instant of time, and with no co-operation of his own beyond this act of faith, from vileness to purity—from a love of evil to a love of good—the sounder, safer and more Scriptural doctrine that, if a man would be saved from the enemies of his soul, he must fight and overcome them in the strength which God gives to all who will ask and receive, is the one now more generally preached to reformed men; and, as a result, the number of those who stand fast in the new life to which they have attained, is steadily increasing.

THE APPETITE FOR DRINK NOT TAKEN AWAY IN A MOMENT.

Still, far too widely in this Gospel work of saving fallen men from the power of appetite, is the delusive idea held out that if a man will "give his heart to Christ," as it is called; that is, pray humbly, sincerely and in faith to have his sins forgiven, and his soul purified from all evil by an application of Divine grace; God will, in answer to this prayer alone, and in an instant of time, take away the appetite for drink which has been for years gradually gaining the mastery over him. We have heard a man declare, in the presence of an assemblage of men who had been slaves to drink, and who were seeking for a way of escape, that God had, in answer to his prayers, destroyed in a moment the appetite which had long held him in a close bondage; and that, if they would come to Him and give Him their hearts, He would work in them the same miracle of spiritual healing. As we listened to his confident speech, we felt how great was the danger in which he himself stood, and how much better it would have been for his hearers if he had kept silent.

HOW MANY ARE REALLY SAVED.

Facts are solid things, and weigh heavily in the scale of argument. They are not always pleasant to look at; but it is weakness to ignore them. Let us take a few facts in connection with this Gospel temperance work. The first of these came to our knowledge while we were revolving the contents of this chapter, and before we had commenced writing it. A leading temperance worker, who was an active participant in the Murphy movement, and who holds that there is for the confirmed drunkard no hope or safety but in the power of religion, stated to us that during the Moody and Sankey revival in Philadelphia, something over two hundred drunken men were reclaimed and converted; changed in heart, as it was declared, and "*saved*" by the power of God. These were gathered together on a certain evening in one of the churches, and the gentleman to whom we have referred was among those who addressed them. The poor, weak, and in too many instances, friendless and homeless men were talked to, and then committed to God in prayer. They had His grace in their hearts—had been "saved" through prayer and faith—and would He not care for, protect and defend them?

Alas, for the sequel! Of all these two hundred converted and "saved" men, who had, in a moment of time, been changed from servants of sensuality and sin into children of God, their souls made "whiter than snow," not over five or six can to-day be found in the ranks of sober men!

In and around Pittsburgh, during the religious temperance revival which, under Francis Murphy, wrought such marvels in that city and neighborhood, over fifty thousand signatures were obtained to the pledge, the signers, in a large number of cases, professing faith in Christ, and having an inner assurance, as they believed, that He would keep them, by the power of His grace, from again falling into the sin and misery of intemperance. But, to-day, only a small proportionate number can be found out of this great multitude who are standing fast by their profession. A like result has followed the great Gospel work of Mr. Murphy in Philadelphia. Of the thirty or forty thousand who signed the pledge and professed to be saved through faith in Christ, the number of men who have been rescued from drunkenness can scarcely be counted by hundreds; and of these the large proportion owe their salvation to the natural safeguards and orderly external conditions which were brought to the aid of spiritual resolve and spiritual forces.

When the excitement of these great revivals was over, and the contagious enthusiasm had died away, and men fell back into their old ways, amid old surroundings and temptations, each alone in the house of his own real life, then came

THE TRIAL AND THE TEST,

and it was found that to depend on grace alone, and the inner change it had effected in answer to prayer, was to rest, too often, in a vain security. The new convert was the same as to the essential evil quality of his life as before his conversion—or turning round to go the other way—and if he stood still where he had turned, and did not, in a new life of practical obedience to Divine laws, walk forward in the Heavenly road, his conversion would avail him nothing. Not that he was left alone by God to stand or fall as he might. No human heart ever felt even the faintest motions of that Divine pity, and compassion, and yearning to save his lost and perishing children, which is felt by our Heavenly Father, who is very love itself. But He cannot save humanity by destroying it, and this destruction would take place the moment he touched man's freedom to choose between good and evil. Of his own will, man has turned away from God; and of his own will he must return to Him if ever he return at all. The way of return has been opened and made plain, and God is forever calling and entreating His poor, wandering ones to come back, and offering them strength to walk, and weapons to fight, and armor for defense. But He cannot walk for them, nor fight for them, nor defend them unless they put on the armor His mercy supplies. They must, of themselves, using the strength He gives them, walk in the Heavenly way; and with the sword of Divine truth He places in their hands, do battle with the enemies of their souls. There is no other means of attaining Heaven. This strength to walk and fight and overcome, is the Divine grace that saves. It is the free gift of our Lord and Saviour Jesus Christ; the very power of God unto salvation.

THE DIVINE GRACE THAT SAVES.

It is by the application of this Divine grace that men are saved from their sins and from the power of hell. But they can never receive it as passive subjects. They must take it and apply it in and of themselves, and use it as if it were their own; yet never forgetting that it is the gift of God, and never ceasing to acknowledge and thank Him for His infinite goodness and mercy in teaching their "hands to war;" in "girding" them "with strength unto the battle," and in giving them a "lamp unto their feet and a light unto their path," so that they may walk in safety.

If salvation were of grace alone, as so many teach in this Gospel temperance work, what need of "sword," or "armor," or a "lamp unto the feet?" for if, in answer to prayer and faith, a man's evil nature is instantly changed, he is no longer subject to temptation, and cannot, therefore, enter into combat with evil; and if God lift him out of the darkness of his carnal nature into the light of regeneration solely in answer to prayer, what need of any lamp unto his feet or light unto his path? He is no longer a pilgrim and a wayfarer, journeying heavenward through an enemy's land.

We press this subject on the reader's attention, because so much of success or failure in this great Gospel temperance work depends on a right understanding of spiritual laws and a true comprehension of the means of salvation. Holding, as we do, that, for the thousands and hundreds of thousands of unhappy and wretched men and women in our land who have become the almost helpless slaves of an appetite which is rarely, if ever, wholly destroyed, no true succor lies in anything but Divine grace and help, we feel that a great responsibility rests with all who, in the providence of God, have been drawn into this work.

Referring to the loose, and we cannot help saying hurtful teachings of too many temperance revivalists, Rev. Charles I. Warren, writing in the New York *Christian Advocate*, says:

"Religious conversion, all are agreed, is the first necessity for all men, and especially for inebriates, as the surest hope of a real and permanent reformation of life. And intemperate men, especially those who become demented rather than demonized, it is well known, are always easily moved by religious influences, even when so drunk that they would wisely be deemed incompetent to execute a will for the disposal of earthly property, and incapable of giving testimony in a court of law.

"Yet, this idea of a spiritual renovation of the heart, while the head is too intoxicated to apprehend a moral obligation, is almost beyond rational belief. It is difficult to conceive that any man, in such a state of voluntarily-induced imbecility, too drunk to hold intelligent converse with men, can be competent to transact business with God, to receive and answer those calls from the Holy Spirit that decide the eternal destinies of the soul."

And he adds: "We judge instinctively that all men, intemperate or sober, must work out their own salvation with fear, while God works in them to will and to do."

This is the key-note to the whole subject of spiritual regeneration. It is active co-operation; work, conflict, victory; and this down on the sphere of common life, and in the midst of temptation—not out of the world, but "in the world;" not something done in and for a man while he waits in prayer on God, but after he has fought his battle with some enemy of his soul, and overcome in the strength which God has given him in answer to prayer. Only they who have fought and conquered can possess the land and dwell there in safety.

AN UNSOUND AND DANGEROUS DOCTRINE.

In a meeting at which we were present, and where from one to two hundred reformed men were gathered for religious worship, and for help and counsel, the hymn commencing

"Prone to wander, Lord I feel it,"

was sung. At its close, a man rose from his seat and entered his protest against the singing of that hymn any more. It is not true, he said, that the man whom God has converted feels any proneness to wander. He had had the grace of God in his soul for—we don't remember how many years—and he could testify that the desire to wander from God's commandments had been wholly removed. He, therefore, repeated his protest against the use of a hymn containing a sentiment so dishonorable to a truly saved Christian. As he sat down, a very young man arose and added the weight of his testimony to the assertion of his older Christian brother. He also, in answer to prayer, as he confidently asserted, had attained unto that higher life which is not only free from sin, but from even the desire to wander from the ways of holiness.

As we looked into and read the faces of these two men, we sighed for what we saw therein, and pitied them for the peril in which they stood. But our greater concern was for the poor, weak, almost helpless ones we saw around us, and for the effect of this delusive error which had been so needlessly thrown into their minds. If any of them should rest in the belief that they, too, had, by the grace of God, been wholly set free from the bondage of sin; that the appetite for drink and the lust of all evil had been extinguished, and their proneness to wander from God taken away in simple answer to prayer, then would their danger, we felt, be so imminent as to leave but little room for hope of their standing in the new life. A stumbling-block had been laid in their way over which they must almost surely fall.

We are writing for the help and safety of men for whom there is but little or no hope of rescue from the depths of evil and sensuality into which they have fallen, except in a truly religious life; not a life of mere faith and sentiment and fancied holiness, but of earnest conflict and daily right living. A life in which not only intemperance is to be shunned as a sin against God, but every impure and evil desire of the heart, and every thought and purpose of wrong to the neighbor. And, believing as we do, that God's grace and power can only be given to those who will take it as active subjects—not mere passive recipients—and by using it as if it were their own, avail themselves of its purifying and regenerating influence, we can do no less than question and reject any doctine that even seems to give a different impression, as delusive and exceedingly dangerous.

To make Gospel temperance the true power of God unto the salvation of intemperate men, we must have in it, and with it, the Gospel of conflict with evil, the Gospel of daily right living, the Gospel of love to the neighbor and the Gospel of common sense. And these are coming more and more into the work, which is widening and increasing, and every year adding thousands upon thousands to the number of those who are saved from the curse of drink.

CHAPTER XV.

TEMPERANCE COFFEE-HOUSES AND FRIENDLY INNS.

THE cure of a drunkard is always attended with peculiar difficulties. The cost is often great. Sometimes cure is found to be impossible. A hundred may be protected from the ravages of intemperance at the cost of saving one who has fallen a victim to the terrible malady. "An ounce of prevention is worth a pound of cure."

While so much is being done to reform and save the drunkard, the work of prevention has not been forgotten. Great good has been accomplished in this direction through the spread of total-abstinence principles. In this the various temperance organizations have done much, and especially with the rising generation. But, so long as men are licensed by the State to sell intoxicating drinks, the net of the tempter is spread on every hand, and thousands of the weak and unwary are yearly drawn therein and betrayed to their ruin. In our great cities a large number of men who have to do business at points remote from their dwellings, are exposed to special temptations. The down-town lunch-room and dining-room have, in most cases, their drinking-bars; or, if no bar is visible, the bill of fare offers, in too many cases, any kind of intoxicating beverage that may be desired. Thousands of men are, in consequence, yearly led away from sobriety.

Seeing this, efforts have been made during the past few years to establish cheap temperance coffee-houses, where workingmen and others may get a good noonday lunch, or a morning and evening meal at a trifling cost. In all cases, these have been found of great service to the cause of temperance. A pint mug of excellent coffee, with sugar and milk, and a large, sweet roll, costing five cents, are found to make a far better and healthier lunch than the highly-seasoned hashes and scraps called "free lunches," which must be washed down by a five or ten-cent glass of liquor.

THE EXPERIMENT IN PHILADELPHIA.

The success which has attended the establishment of cheap temperance coffee-houses in this city (Philadelphia), is quite remarkable. In the fall of 1874, Joshua L. Baily, one of our active, clear-headed merchants, who had been for many years an earnest temperance man, determined to give the cheap coffee-house experiment a fair trial, cost what it might; for he saw that if it could be made successful, it would be a powerful agency in the work of prevention. He began in a modest way, taking a small store at the corner of Market and Fifteenth Streets, and fitting it up in a neat and attractive manner. With a few pounds of coffee, and a few dozens of rolls, the place was opened, the single attendant, a woman, acting the double part of cook and waiter. For five cents a pint mug of the best Java coffee, with milk and sugar, and a good-sized roll, were furnished.

From the very start "The Workingmen's Central Coffee-House," as Mr. Baily called it, was successful. In the immediate neighborhood five hundred workmen were employed on the city buildings, and opposite stood the Pennsylvania Railroad freight depot, to which came daily about the same number of men—draymen, teamsters and others. It took but a few days to so crowd the new coffee-room at the usual lunching time as to require an additional assistant. From day to day the business went on increasing, until more help and larger accommodations became necessary. Soon a complete kitchen had to be built in the basement, and the adjoining store added, in order to meet the steadily-enlarging demands upon the new establishment. The fame of the good coffee, which was better than most people found at home, spread far and near, and larger and larger numbers of clerks, workingmen and others, turned their steps daily, at lunch time, towards the Central Coffee-House. It was so much better than the poor stuff served in most of the eating-houses; and, with the sweet roll added, so much better than the free lunch and glass of beer or whisky with which too many had been accustomed to regale themselves.

SIGNAL SUCCESS.

Steadily swelled the tide of custom. Within a year a third store, adjoining, was added. But the enlarged premises soon proved inadequate to the accommodation of the still-increasing crowd.

At this writing "The Central" is from six to seven times larger than when first opened; and there lunch in its rooms, daily, nearly two thousand persons. One room has been fitted up for ladies exclusively, in which from forty to fifty can lunch at one time.

But Mr. Baily looked beyond the cheap coffee and rolls by which he was able to keep so many away from bar-rooms and restaurants where liquor was sold. He believed in other influences and safeguards. And to this end, and at his own cost, he fitted up the various rooms over the seven stores extending along Market Street from Fifteenth to Broad, in which the coffee-rooms are located, and set them apart for various uses. Here is a lecture-hall, capable of seating four hundred persons; a free reading-room, well warmed and lighted and supplied with the best daily newspapers, American and English illustrated publications, and the standard periodicals; besides four other rooms that will hold from seventy to one hundred persons, which are used for various meeting purposes, all in connection with temperance. Five regular services are held in the lecture-room every week, viz.: "Bible Reading," on Sunday afternoon; "Temperance Experience meeting," on Monday evening; "Prayer and Praise meeting," Tuesday evening; "Gospel Temperance meeting," on Thursday evening; and "Youths' Temperance meeting," Friday evening. These meetings are often crowded, and, like the coffee-rooms below, attract audiences made up from every rank in society. At many of these meetings, Mr. Baily presides in person.

Encouraged by the success of this first effort, Mr. Baily opened another cheap coffee-house in the very centre of the wholesale trade of the city, where thousands of clerks, workingmen and merchants were in the habit of resorting for lunch or dinner to the restaurants and bar-rooms in the neighborhood. This, located at No. 31 South Fourth Street, he called "The Model Coffee-House."

CROWDED FROM THE FIRST.

From the first it was crowded even to an uncomfortable extent. The demands of its patrons soon rendered larger quarters a necessity. A new building was erected specially adapted to the purpose, many novel features being introduced which a twelvemonth's experience had suggested.

The *new* "Model" opened June 1st, 1876. Many persons thought it was too large, and that it would never be filled. But it was thronged on the day of opening, and on every day since the demands upon it have been fully up to its capacity. The number lunching here daily is about three thousand.

In the establishment of the coffee-houses there were, of course, many mistakes, the results of inexperience. Many things had to be unlearned as well as many learned. But mistakes were promptly corrected. With the growth of the work, ability to provide for it seemed to keep pace, and modifications in the management were adopted as necessity dictated. Not much was anticipated at the commencement beyond furnishing a mug of coffee and a roll of bread, but it soon became apparent that something more than this was needed. To meet this necessity, the coffee-house bill of fare was greatly extended, and now quite a variety of nutritious and substantial dishes are provided, and each at the uniform price of *five cents.* The main feature—the coffee—is, however, preserved. A full pint mug of the best Java (equal to two ordinary cups) with pure, rich milk and white sugar, and two ounces of either wheat or brown bread, all for *five cents,* is the every-day lunch of many a man who, but for this provision, would be found in the dram-shop.

No dish, as we have said, costs over five cents, which is the standard price the year round, whatever the fluctuations of markets may be. In addition to the bread and coffee already mentioned for five cents, the bill of fare comprises puddings of rice, tapioca and corn starch, baked apples dressed with sugar and milk, all sorts of pies (half a pie being given for a portion), mushes of cracked wheat, corn and oatmeal. dumplings, eggs, potatoes, beans, ham, corned beef, liver, "scrapple," sausage, custards, soups, pickles and, in season, fresh fruits. Of bread, there are Boston and Philadelphia brown, wheat, Philadelphia and Vienna rolls. A pint glass of milk with a roll, costs five cents; butter three cents, and extra rolls one cent each; so that for ten or fifteen cents a man gets a full luncheon, as every portion of food is equal to a large saucer heaped.

These establishments require, of course, the most methodical, orderly and careful management, with capable matrons at the head of each, and a steward or superintendent to make intelligent purchases. At the "Model Coffee-House," there are nearly fifty employees, and, excepting three or four men, they are girls and women. The upper rooms of the building are for the lodgings, offices, laundry and drawing-room, for the use of the employees. The girls, who are mostly of country birth and training, are thus furnished with a good and safe home, where they have books and music, large and well-furnished chambers, a good table—they dine at one family table in their own dining-room—and have their washing and ironing done in the house. They are required to be neat and tidy in appearance, respectable and discreet in character and manner.

THE GOOD DONE.

The good that is done through an instrumentality like this can never be fully known. Of those who are drawn into paths of safety, we do not so often hear as of those who are led astray. But enough is already known of the good done by these two coffee-houses to give large encouragement for their establishment in other localities and other cities. Hundreds of young men who had fallen into the dangerous habit of taking a glass of beer every day with their lunch, now take a fragrant cup of coffee instead, and find themselves better for the change; hundreds more who had begun to feel the insidious encroachments of appetite, have been able to get out of the way of temptation.

The question that naturally arises with all who look practically at this matter is, whether there is any profit in the business of keeping a cheap temperance coffee-house? Can a pint of coffee, with sugar, milk and a two-ounce roll of bread, be furnished for five cents and leave any margin for profit? Mr. Baily's experiment has proved that it can.

FRIENDLY INNS.

But not alone in Philadelphia is the cheap coffee-house to be found. There are hundreds of them in our various towns and cities, though none on so large a scale as here; and they are rapidly multiplying and doing good. "The Friendly Inn," and "The Holly-Tree Inn," are places somewhat similar in character, but partaking more of the nature of an "inn" than a simple eating-house. These have, usually, a pleasant parlor, with light, and warmth, and books, into which any one may come and pass the evening, instead of drifting into a saloon, and where cheap meals and lodgings can be had if needed. In Cleveland, Ohio, Christian temperance work, which is very large and effective, is carried on almost entirely in connection with "Friendly Inns," of which there are five. A chapel, reading-room, sleeping apartments and a cheap restaurant are maintained in connection with each of these inns. The women engaged in the cause of Gospel temperance in that city regard them as most valuable auxiliaries to the spiritual work in which they are engaged. In a large number of cases, they have been the direct means of bringing men in whom few traces of goodness could at first be discerned in such contact with religious influences as to win them over to a better life.

CHAPTER XVI.

TEMPERANCE LITERATURE.

THE greatest and most effective agency in any work of enlightenment and reform is the press. By it the advanced thinker and Christian philanthropist is able to speak to the whole people, and to instruct, persuade and influence them. He can address the reason and conscience of thousands, and even of hundreds of thousands of people to whom he could never find access in any other way, and so turn their minds to the right consideration of questions of social interest in regard to which they had been, from old prejudices or habits of thinking, in doubt or grievous error.

No cause has been more largely indebted to the press than that of temperance reform. From the very beginning of agitation on the subject of this reform, the press has been used with great efficiency; and to-day, the literature of temperance is a force of such magnitude and power, that it is moving whole nations, and compelling Parliaments, Chambers of Deputies and Houses of Congress to consider the claims of a question which, if presented fifty years ago, would have been treated, in these grave assemblages, with levity or contempt.

For many years after the reform movement began in this country, the press was used with marked effect. But as most of the books, pamphlets and tracts which were issued came through individual enterprise, the editions were often small and the prices high; and as the sale of such publications was limited, and the profit, if any, light, the efforts to create a broad and comprehensive temperance literature met with but feeble encouragement. But in 1865, a convention was called to meet at Saratoga to consider the subject of a national organization so comprehensive and practical that all the friends of temperance in religious denominations and temperance organizations could unite therein for common work. Out of this convention grew the

NATIONAL TEMPERANCE SOCIETY AND PUBLICATION HOUSE,

which began, at once, the creation of a temperance literature worthy of the great cause it represented. The president of this society is Hon. William E. Dodge, of New York. The vice-presidents are ninety-two in number, and include some of the most distinguished men in the country; clergymen, jurists, statesmen, and private citizens eminent for their public spirit and philanthropy. It has now been in existence some twelve years. Let us see what it has done in that time for temperance literature and the direction and growth of a public sentiment adverse to the liquor traffic. We let the efficient corresponding secretary and publishing agent, J. N. Stearns, speak for the association he so ably represents. Its rooms are at No. 58 Reade Street, New York. Referring to the initial work of the society, "It was resolved," says Mr. Stearns, "that the publishing agent should keep 'all the temperance literature of the day.' This was found to consist of less than a dozen different publications in print, and these of no special value. All the plates of valuable works before in existence were either shipped across the water or melted up and destroyed. The society commenced at once to create a literature of its own, but found it was not the work of a moment. The first publication outside of its monthly paper, was a four-page tract by Rev. T. L. Cuyler, D.D., in February, 1866, entitled 'A Shot at the Decanter,' of which about two hundred thousand copies have been published.

FIRST BOOK PUBLISHED.

"The first book was published in May of the same year, entitled, 'Scripture Testimony against Intoxicating Wine.' Prizes were offered for the best tracts and books, and the best talent in the land sought and solicited to aid in giving light upon every phase of the question. The result has been that an immense mass of manuscripts have been received, examined, assorted, some approved and many rejected, and the list of publications has gone on steadily increasing, until in the eleven years it amounts to four hundred and fifty varieties upon every branch of the temperance question. There were over twenty separate so-called secret temperance societies, each with a different ritual and constitution, with subordinate organizations scattered all over the land. These contained probably about one million of members. Then there were churches, open societies, State temperance unions, etc., each operating independently and with no common bond of union. Some were for moral suasion alone, others for political action, while others were for both united. The great need for some national organization which should be a common centre and ground of union, a medium of communication between all, and to aid, strengthen and benefit every existing organization and denomination, was felt all over the land.

"This society was organized to supply such a need. It is both a society and a publication house. The need and demand came from every quarter for facts, statistics, arguments and appeals upon every phase of the question, in neat, cheap and compact form, which could be sent everywhere and used by everybody. Public opinion had settled down against us, and light was needed to arouse it to right action. The pulpit and the platform were to be supplemented by the press, which, henceforth, was to be used in this great and rapidly strengthening cause, as in every other, to reach the individuals and homes of every portion of the land.

AFTER TWELVE YEARS.

"Twelve years have passed—years of anxious preparation and toil, of seed-planting and sowing, and they have been improved. This society now publishes books and tracts upon the moral, economical, physiological, political, financial, religious, medical and social phases of the reform. We have the writings of over two hundred different persons in almost every walk and station in life. We already have a literature of no mean character. Its influence is not only felt in every State and Territory in the land, but in every country on the globe.

* * * * * * * *

"Among the early publications of the society were those printed upon 'The Adulteration of Liquors,' 'The Physiological Action of Alcohol,' 'Alcohol: Its Nature and Effects,' 'Alcohol: Its Place and Power,' 'Is Alcohol Food?' 'Text-Book of Temperance,' etc., followed later by 'Bacchus Dethroned,' 'The Medical Use of Alcohol,' 'Is Alcohol a Neccessary of Life?' 'Our Wasted Resources,' 'On Alcohol,' 'Prohibition does Prohibit,' 'Fruits of the Liquor Traffic,' 'The Throne of Iniquity,' 'Suppression of the Liquor Traffic,' 'Alcohol as a Food and Medicine,' etc.

"The truths of these books and pamphlets, which have been reproduced in a thousand ways in sermons, addresses, newspapers, etc., have already permeated the community to such an extent as to bear much fruit."

In the creation of a literature for children, the society early issued *The Youths' Temperance Banner*, a paper for Sunday-schools. This has attained a circulation of nearly one hundred and fifty thousand copies monthly. It has also created a Sunday-school temperance library, which numbers already as many as seventy bound volumes; editions of which reaching in the aggregate to one hundred and eighty-three thousand five hundred and seventy-six volumes have already been sold. The society also publishes a monthly paper called the *National Temperance Advocate*, which has a wide circulation.

REMARKABLE GROWTH OF TEMPERANCE LITERATURE.

The number of books, pamphlets and tracts which have been issued by the National Temperance Society during the twelve years of its existence, is four hundred and sixty, some of them large and important volumes.

To this extraordinary production and growth of temperance literature in the past twelve years are the people indebted for that advanced public sentiment which is to-day gathering such force and will.

And here, let us say, in behalf of a society which has done such grand and noble work, that from the very outset it has had to struggle with pucuniary difficulties.

Referring to the difficulties and embarrassments with which the society has had to contend from the beginning, the secretary says:

"The early financial struggles of the society are known only to a very few persons. It was deemed best by the majority of the board not to let the public know our poverty. Looking back over the eleven years of severe struggles, pecuniary embarrassments, unexpected difficulties, anxious days, toiling, wearisome nights, with hopes of relief dashed at almost every turn, surrounded by the indifference of friends, and with the violent opposition of enemies, we can only wonder that the society has breasted the storm and is saved from a complete and total wreck. * * * This society never was endowed, never had a working capital, never has been the recipient of contributions from churches or of systematic donations from individuals. It never has had a day of relief from financial embarrassment since its organization; and yet there never has been a day but that the sum of ten thousand dollars would have lifted it out of its embarrassments and started it with a buoyant heart on towards the accomplishment of its mission."

And he adds: "Notwithstanding all these constant and ever-pressing financial embarrassments, the society has never faltered for one moment, but has gone steadily on doing its appointed work, exploring new fields, and developing both old and new truths and documents and principles, and it stands to-day the strongest and most solid and substantial bulwark against intemperance in the land."

A MOST IMPORTANT AGENCY.

As the most important of all the agencies now used for the suppression of the liquor traffic, and as the efficient ally of all let us rally to the support of our great publication house and see that it has ampler means for the work in which it is engaged. There are hundreds of thousands of men and women in our land who are happy and prosperous to-day because of what this society has done in the last twelve years to create a sentiment adverse to the traffic and to the drinking usages of society. Its work is so silent and unobtrusive in comparison with that of many other efficient, but more limited instrumentalities, that we are apt to lose sight of its claims, and to fail in giving an adequate support to the very power, which is, in a large measure, the source of power to all the rest.

If we would war successfully with our strong and defiant enemy, we must look to it that the literature of temperance does not languish. We are not making it half as efficient as it might be. Here we have a thoroughly organized publication house, with capable and active agents, which, if the means were placed at its disposal, could flood the country with books, pamphlets and tracts by millions every year; and we leave it to struggle with embarrassments, and to halting and crippled work. This is not well. Our literature is our right arm in this great conflict, and only in the degree that we strengthen this arm will we be successful in our pursuit of victory.

FINANCIAL VIEW OF THE LICENSE SYSTEM.

"Whatever revenue license pays the State is fully counterbalanced by the increased cost of jails, poorhouses and police, for which the patient public pays immense taxation. The moral burdens from the infamous traffic are all additional to the financial."

CHAPTER XVII.

LICENSE A FAILURE AND A DISGRACE.

FOR over two hundred years in this country, and for a much longer period of time in Great Britain and some of the countries of Continental Europe, attempts have been made to protect the people against the evils of intemperance by restrictive liquor laws. But as these laws were permissive and not prohibitory, the evil was not restrained. Nay, its larger growth came as the natural consequence of such laws, for they not only gave to a few men in every community the right to live and grow rich by doing all in their power to increase the evil, but threw around them the protection of the State; so leaving the people powerless in their hands.

HISTORY OF LICENSE IN MASSACHUSETTS.

The history of all restrictive laws which have stopped short of absolute prohibition, is a history of the saddest of failures, and shows that to license an evil is to increase its power.

Judge Robert C. Pitman, in his "Alcohol and the State," an exceedingly valuable discussion of the "Problem of Law as Applied to the Liquor Traffic," gives an instructive history of the license laws of

Massachusetts from early colonial times down to the year 1877. The experience of Massachusetts is that of every other community, State or nation, which has sought to repress drunkenness and its attendant evils by the enactment of license laws; and we ask the reader's earnest and candid consideration of the facts we shall here present.

As early as 1636, an effort was made in the Old Colony to lessen intemperance by the passage of a restrictive law, declaring "That none be suffered to retail wine, strong water or beer, either within doors or without, except in inns or victualing-houses allowed." That this law did not lessen the evil of drunkenness is plain from the fact that, in 1646, in the preamble to a new liquor law it was declared by the Massachusetts colony that, "Forasmuch as drunkenness is a vice to be abhorred of all nations, especially of those who hold out and profess the Gospel of Christ, and seeing *any strict law will not prevail unless the cause be taken away*, it is, therefore, ordered by this Court,"—What? Entire prohibition of the sale of intoxicating drinks? No. Only, "That no merchant, cooper or any other person whatever, shall, after the first day of the first month, sell any wine under one-quarter of a cask, neither by quart, gallon or any other measure, *but only such taverners as are licensed to sell by the gallon.*" And in order still further to protect and encourage the publican in his vested and exclusive right, it was further enacted that, "Any *taverners* or other persons who shall inform against any transgressor, shall have one-half of the fines for his *encouragement.*" This law contained a section which forbids any person licensed "to sell strong waters, or any private housekeeper to permit any person to sit drinking or tippling strong waters, wine or strong beer in their houses."

THE EVIL STILL INCREASING.

Still the evil of drunkenness went on increasing under the license system, until in 1692, we find in a preamble to certain more stringent laws for the regulation of the traffic, this sad confession: "And forasmuch as the ancient, true and principal use of inns, taverns, ale-houses, victualing-houses and other houses for common entertainment is for receipt, relief and lodging of travelers and strangers, and the refreshment of persons on lawful business. * * * And not for entertainment and harboring of lewd or idle people to spend or consume their time or money there; therefore, *to prevent the mischief and great disorders happening daily by abuse of such houses,* It is further enacted," etc.—not prohibition of the sale; but further restrictions and penalties. How far these restrictions and penalties were effective, appears from the statue of 1695, in the preamble of which is a complaint that divers persons who had obtained license to sell liquor to be taken away and not drunk in their houses, did, notwithstanding, "give entertainment to persons to sit drinking and tippling there," while others who "*have no license at all* are yet so hardy as to run upon the law," to the "great increase of drunkenness and other debaucheries."

These colonial fathers, in their efforts to lessen the evil of drinking by restrictive license, for which a fee to the State was required, opened a door for the unlicensed dram-shop, which was then, as it is now, one of the worst forms of the liquor traffic, because it is in the hands of more unscrupulous persons, too many of whom are of the lowest and vilest class, and whose tippling-houses are dens of crime and infamy as well as drunkenness.

How this was in the colony of Massachusetts under license in 1695 is seen above, and further appears in this recital taken from the statute to further limit the spread of drunkenness, wherein it refers to "divers *ill-disposed and indigent persons, the pains and penalties in the laws already made not regarding*, who are so hardy *as to presume to sell and retail* strong beer, ale, cider, sherry wine, rum or other strong liquors or mixed drinks, and *to keep common tippling-houses*, thereby harboring and entertaining apprentices, Indians, negroes and other idle and dissolute persons, tending to the ruin and impoverishment of families, and all impieties and debaucheries, and *if detected are unable to pay their fine*." All such were sentenced to the whipping-post.

Three years later, the curse of the licensed traffic had so augmented that another effort was made for its regulation by the enactment of a new and more comprehensive law entitled, "An Act for the Inspecting and *Suppressing of Disorders* in Licensed Houses."

WORSE AND WORSE.

How successful the good people of Massachusetts were in holding in check and regulating the evil which they had clothed with power by license, appears in the preamble to a new Act passed in 1711, "For reclaiming the over great number of licensed houses, many of which are chiefly used for revelling and tippling, and become *nurseries of intemperance and debauchery*, indulged by the masters and keepers of the same for the sake of gain."

So it went on, from bad to worse, under the Colonial Government, until 1787, when the State constitution was adopted. To what a frightful magnitude the evil of drunkenness, provided for and fostered by license, had grown, appears from an entry in the diary of John Adams, under date of February 29th, 1760, in which he says that few things were "so fruitful of destructive evils" as "licensed houses." They had become, he declares, "the eternal haunts of loose, disorderly people of the town, which renders them offensive and unfit for the entertainment of any traveler of the least delicacy." * * * "Young people are tempted to waste their time and money, and to acquire habits of intemperance and idleness, that we often see reduce many to beggary and vice, and lead some of them, at least, to prison and the gallows."

In entering upon her career as a State, Massachusetts continued the license system, laying upon it many prudent restrictions, all of which were of no avail, for the testimony is complete as to the steady increase of drunkenness, crime and debauchery.

TESTIMONY OF JOHN ADAMS.

Writing to Mr. Rush in 1811, John Adams says: "Fifty-three years ago I was fired with a zeal, amounting to enthusiasm, against ardent spirits, the multiplication of taverns, retailers, dram-shops and tippling-houses. Grieved to the heart to see the number of idlers, thieves, sots and consumptive patients made for the physicians in these infamous seminaries, I applied to the Court of Sessions, procured a Committee of Inspection and Inquiry, reduced the number of licensed houses, etc., *but I only acquired the reputation of a hypocrite and an ambitious demagogue by it.* The number of licensed houses was soon reinstated; drams, grog and sotting were not diminished, *and remain to this day as deplorable as ever.*"

OPENING A WIDER DOOR.

In 1816, so demoralized had the sentiment of the people become, and so strong the liquor interest of the State, that the saving provision in the license laws, which limited the sale of liquor to inns and taverns, was repealed, and licenses were granted to common victualers, "who shall not be required to furnish accommodations" for travelers; and also to confectioners on the same terms as to inn-keepers; that is, to sell and to be drunk on the premises. This change in the license laws of Massachusetts was declared, by Judge Aldrich, in 1867, to be "one of the most fruitful sources of crime and vice that ever existed in this Commonwealth."

Up to as late as 1832, attempts were continued to patch up and amend the license laws of the State; after that they were left, for a time, to do their evil work, all efforts to make them anything but promoters of drunkenness, crime and poverty being regarded as fruitless.

"Miserable in principle," says Judge Pitman, "license laws were found no less inefficient in practice." Meantime, the battle against the liquor traffic had been going on in various parts of the State. In 1835, a law was secured by which the office of county commissioner (the licensing authority) was made an elective office; heretofore it had been held by appointment. This gave the people of each county a local control over the liquor question, and in the very first year the counties of Plymouth and Bristol elected boards committed to the policy of no license. Other counties followed this good example; and to bar all questions of the right to refuse every license by a county, the power was expressly conferred by a law passed in 1837.

A CHANGE FOR THE BETTER.

The good results were immediately apparent in all places where license to sell intoxicating drinks was refused. After a thorough investigation of the matter, the Judiciary Committee of the Legislature reported the evidence to be "perfectly incontrovertable, that the good order and the physical and moral welfare of the community had been promoted by refusing to license the sale of ardent spirits; and that although the laws have been and are violated to some extent in different places, the practice soon becomes disreputable and hides itself from the public eye by shrinking into obscure and dark places; that noisy and tumultuous assemblies in the streets and public quarrels cease where license is refused; *and that pauperism has very rapidly diminished from the same cause.*"

An attempt to prohibit entirely the retail liquor traffic was made in 1838, by the passage of what was known as the "Fifteen-Gallon Law," which forbade the sale of spirituous liquors in a less quantity than fifteen gallons, which had to be "carried away all at one time;" except by apothecaries and practicing physicians, who might sell for use in the arts and for medicinal purposes.

But this law remained in operation only a year and a half; when, in concession to the liquor interest of the State, which had been strong enough to precipitate a political revolution and get its own men in the legislature, it was repealed.

"But the State," says Judge Pitman, "while the memory of license was fresh, was not to fall again under its sway. The struggle for local prohibition was at once renewed, and in a few years license had ceased throughout the Commonwealth. The statement may surprise many; but I have the authority of the city clerk of Boston for saying, that 'no licenses for the sale of intoxicating liquors were granted in Boston between 1841 and 1852.' * * * And so the chapter of license was apparently closed. It had not only had its 'day,' but its centuries in court; and the well-nigh unanimous verdict was: '*disgrace—failure.*'"

So strong was this conviction in the minds of the people of Massachusetts, that Governor Bullock, in 1861, while acting as chairman of the Judiciary Committee of the House, gave it expression in these notable words: "It may be taken as the solemnly declared judgment of the people of the Commonwealth, that the principle of licensing the traffic in intoxicating drinks as a beverage, *and thus giving legal sanction to that which is regarded in itself as an evil, is no longer admissible in morals or in legislation.*"

THE LIQUOR POWER IN THE ASCENDANT AGAIN.

But in 1868, adverse influences prevailed, and after all her sad and disgraceful experience, Massachusetts abandoned her prohibition of the traffic and went back to license again; but the evil consequences began to show themselves so quickly that the law was repealed in less than a year.

Governor Claflin, in his message to the legislature in January, 1869, thus speaks of the effect of the new license law: "The increase of drunkenness and crime during the last six months, as compared with the same period of 1867, is very marked and decisive as to the operation of the law. *The State prisons, jails and houses of correction are being rapidly filled,* and will soon require enlarged accommodation if the commitments continue to increase as they have since the present law went in force."

While the chaplain of the State prison in his annual report for 1868, says: "The prison never was so full as at the present time. If the rapidly increasing tide of intemperance, so greatly swollen by the present wretched license law, is suffered to rush on unchecked, there will be a fearful increase of crime, and the State must soon extend the limits of the prison, or create another."

This law was repealed, as we have seen. A year of its bitter fruit was enough for the people.

SUBMITTING AGAIN TO THE YOKE.

But, strange to say, after all she has suffered from license laws, the old Bay State has again submitted to the yoke, and is once more in the hands of the great liquor interest. In 1874, she drifted out from the safe harbor of prohibition, and we find her, to-day, on the stormy and storm-wrecked sea of license. A miserable attempt has been made by the friends of this law to show that its action has been salutory in Boston, the headquarters of the liquor power, in the diminution of dram-shops and arrests for drunkenness. Water may run up hill in Boston; but it obeys the law of gravitation in other places. We leave the reader to draw his own conclusions from this extract from the report of the License Commissioners of that city, made February 1st, 1877: "It must be admitted that the business of liquor-selling in this city is, to a very large extent, in the hands of *irresponsible men and women,* whose idea of a license law ends with the simple matter of paying a certain sum, the amount making but little difference to them, *provided they are left to do as they please after payment.* Besides the saloons and bar-rooms, which are open publicly, the traffic in small grocery stores, in cellars and in dwelling-houses, in some parts of the city, *is almost astounding. The Sunday trade is enormous, and it seems as if there were not hours enough in the whole round of twenty-four, or days enough in the entire week to satisfy the dealers.*"

The experience of Massachusetts is, as we have already said, the experience of every community, State or nation in which an effort has been made to abridge the evils of intemperance by licensing the dram-shop.

And to whom and to what class of citizens does the State accord, under license, the privilege of making gain out of the people's loss? For whom is every interest in the nation taxed and every industry hurt? For whom are the houses of the poor made poorer; and the supply of bread diminished? For whom are a crime-assaulted and pauper-ridden people driven to build jails and poor-houses, and insane asylums, and maintain courts and juries and a vast army of police, at the cost of millions of dollars every year?

For great benefactors to whom the nation owes a debt of gratitude? For men who are engaged in great industrial or commercial enterprises? Promoters of education? leaders in the great march of civilization? Even if this were so, better not to have accepted the service than pay for it at so fearful a cost.

Who and what are these men?—this great privileged class? Let us see. In Boston, we have the testimony of the License Commissioners that liquor-selling is in the hands of "irresponsible men and women," who pay a license for the privilege of doing "as they please after payment." And for the maintenance of these "irresponsible" men and women in their right to corrupt and degrade the people, a forced tax is laid on every bit of property and every interest in the great city of Boston! What was the tax on tea to this? And yet, Boston patiently submits!

Is it better in New York, Philadelphia, Baltimore, Cincinnati, Chicago or any other of our large cities? Not a whit! In some it is worse, even, than in the capital of the old Bay State. In one of these last-mentioned cities, where, under the license system so dear to politicians, and for which they are chiefly responsible, between seven and eight thousand places in which liquor is sold at retail exist, an effort was made in 1876 to ascertain the character and antecedents of every person engaged in dram-selling. We are not able to say how carefully or thoroughly the investigation was pursued, but it was in the hands of those who meant that it should be complete and accurate. One fact elicited was, that the proportion of native-born citizens to the whole number engaged in the business was less than one-sixth. Another was, that over six thousand of these dram-sellers belonged to the criminal class, and had suffered imprisonment, some for extended terms in the State prison. And another was, that nearly four thousand of the drinking-places which had been established under the fostering care of State license laws were houses of ill-fame as well! Comment is unnecessary.

We cannot lessen the evil nor abate the curse of drunkenness so long as we license a traffic, which, from its essential hostility to all the best interests of society, naturally falls into the hands of our worst citizens, who persistently violate every salutory and restrictive feature in the laws which give their trade a recognized existence.

What then? Is there any remedy short of Prohibition? We believe not.

CHAPTER XVIII.

PROHIBITION.

IT has taken nearly half a century to convince the people that only in total abstinence lies any hope of cure for the drunkard. When this doctrine was first announced, its advocates met with opposition, ridicule and even insult. Now it has almost universal acceptance. The effort to hold an inebriate's appetite in check by any restriction that included license, has, in all cases, proved so signal a failure, that the "letting down," or "tapering off" process has been wholly abandoned in inebriate asylums. There is no hope, as we have said, but in complete abstinence.

NO REMEDY BUT PROHIBITION.

Is there any other means of cure for national drunkenness? The remedy of license has been found as valueless for the whole people as restriction for the individual. Appetite, when once depraved, becomes, in the individual, lawless, exacting and unscrupulous; not hesitating to trample on duty, justice, humanity and every public and private virtue. It will keep no faith; it will hold to no pledge, however solemnly taken. It must be wholly denied or it will be wholly master.

As in the individual, so in the nation, State or community. Appetite loses nothing by aggregation; nor are the laws of its action changed. If not denied by prohibition in the State, as by total abstinence in the individual, it will continue to entail upon the people loss and ruin and unutterable woes. License, restrictive permission, tax, all will be vain in the future as they have been in the past. There is no hope, no help, no refuge in anything but *Prohibition!*

And here we art met by two questions, fairly and honestly asked. First. Is prohibition right in the abstract as a legislative measure? Second. Can prohibitory laws be enforced, and will they cure the evil of drunkenness?

First, as to the question of legislative action. Can the State forbid the sale of intoxicating drinks as a beverage without violating the natural right of certain citizens, engaged in the manufacture and sale of these articles, to supply them to customers who wish to purchase?

We answer, that no man has a natural right to do wrong; that is, to engage in any pursuit by which he makes gain out of loss and injury to his neighbor. The essential principle of government is the well-being of the people. It guarantees to the weak, security against the strong; it punishes evil-doers, and seeks to protect its citizens from the evil effects of that unscrupulous selfishness in the individual which would trample on the rights of all the rest in its pursuit of money or power.

Now, if it can be shown that the liquor traffic is a good thing; that it benefits the people; makes them more prosperous and happy; improves their health; promotes education and encourages virtue, then its right to exist in the community has been established. Or, even if the good claimed for it be only negative instead of positive, its right must still be unquestioned. But what if it works evil and only evil in the State? What if it blights and curses every neighborhood, and town, and city, and nation in which it exists; laying heavy taxes upon the people that it may live and flourish, crippling all industries; corrupting the morals of the people; enticing the young from virtue; filling jails, and poor-houses, and asylums with a great army of criminals, paupers and insane men and women, yearly extinguishing the light in thousands of happy homes? What then?

Does this fruit of the liquor traffic establish its right to existence and to the protection of law? Let the reader answer the question for himself. That it entails all of these evils, and many more, upon the community, cannot and will not be denied. That it does any good, cannot be shown. Fairly, then, it has no right to existence in any government established for the good of the people; and in suppressing it, no wrong can be done.

PROHIBITION NOT UNCONSTITUTIONAL.

How the question of prohibition is regarded by the highest legal authority in the United States will appear from the following opinions officially given by four of the Justices of our Supreme Court. They are expressed in no doubtful or hesitating form of speech:

Chief Justice Taney said: "If any State deems the retail and internal traffic in ardent spirits injurious to its citizens, and calculated to produce idleness, vice or debauchery, I see nothing in the Constitution of the United States to prevent it from regulating or restraining the traffic, or from prohibiting it altogether, if it thinks proper."—[5 Howard, 577.]

Hon. Justice McLean said: "A license to sell is a matter of police and revenue within the power of the State."—[5 Ibid., 589.] "If the foreign article be injurious to the health and morals of the community, a State may prohibit the sale of it."

Hon. Justice Catron said: "If the State has the power of restraint by license to any extent, she may go to the length of prohibiting sales altogether."—[5 Ibid., 611.]

Hon. Justice Grier said: "It is not necessary to array the appalling statistics of misery, pauperism and crime which have their origin in the use and abuse of ardent spirits. The police power, which is exclusively in the State, is competent to the correction of these great evils, and all measures of restraint or prohibition necessary to effect that purpose are within the scope of that authority."—[Ibid., 532.]

That the State has a clear right to prohibit the

sale of intoxicating drinks, because this sale not only hurts all other interests, but destroys the health and degrades the morals of the people, has been fully shown.

The question next to be considered is, Can prohibitory laws be enforced? and if so, will they remove from the people the curse of drunkenness?

CAN PROHIBITORY LAWS BE ENFORCED?

As to the complete enforcement of any salutory law, that depends mainly on the public sentiment regarding it, and on the organized strength of its opposers. If the common sentiment of the people were in favor of every man's liberty to steal whatever he could lay his hands on, it would be found very difficult to convict a rogue, no matter how clearly expressed the law against stealing. A single thief in the jury-box could defeat the ends of justice. A hundred loop-holes for escape can always be found in the provisions of a law with which the majority of the people are not in sympathy. Indeed, it often happens that such loop-holes are provided by the law-makers themselves; and this is especially true in too many of the laws made for the suppression of the liquor trade.

Is this an argument against the enactment of laws to protect the people from great wrongs—especially the weaker and more helpless ones? To the half-hearted, the indifferent and the pusillanimous—yes! But with brave, true men, who have at heart the best interests of humanity, this can only intensify opposition to wrong, and give strength for new efforts to destroy its power. These have an undying faith in the ultimate victory of good over evil, and mean, so far as they are concerned, that the battle shall continue until that victory is won.

Judge Pitman has eloquently expressed this sentiment in the closing pages of his recent work, to which we have more than once referred. Speaking of those who distrust the practicability of securing such legislation as will effectually destroy the liquor trade, he says: "They are appalled at the power of the traffic. They see that it has uncounted wealth at its command; that it is organized and unscrupulous; that it has the support of fierce appetite behind it and the alliance of every evil lust; that it is able to bribe or intimidate the great political parties. All this is true; but still it is not to be the final victor. It has all the elemental moral forces of the human race against it, and though their working be slow, and their rate of progress dependent on human energy and fidelity, the ultimate result is as certain as the action of the law of gravity in the material universe. Wealth may be against us; rank may affect to despise us; but the light whose dawn makes a new morning in the world, rarely shines from palace or crown, but from the manger and the cross. Before the aroused consciences of the people, wielding the indomitable will of a State, the destroyers of soul and body shall go down forever."

THE VALUE OF PROHIBITORY LAWS WHEN ENFORCED.

It remains now to show how far prohibitory laws, when enforced, have secured the end for which they were created. On this point, the evidence is clear and satisfactory. In Vermont, a prohibitory law has existed for over twenty-three years. In some parts of the State it is rigidly enforced; in others with less severity. Judge Peck, of the Supreme Court says: "The law has had an effect upon our customs, and has done away with that of treating and promiscuous drinking. * * * *In attending court for ten years, I do not remember to have seen a drunken man.*" In St. Johnsbury, where there is a population of five thousand, the law has been strictly enforced; and the testimony in regard to the town is this: "There is no bar, no dram-shop, no poor, and no policeman walks the streets. It is the workingman's paradise."

Connecticut enacted a prohibitory law in 1854. In 1855, Governor Dutton said, in his annual message to the General Assembly: "There is scarcely an open grog-shop in the State, the jails are fast becoming tenantless, and a delightful air of security is everywhere enjoyed."

In Meriden, the chaplain of the reform school testified that "crime had diminished seventy-five per cent." In New London, the jail was tenantless. In Norwich, the jails and almshouses were reported "as almost empty." But in 1873, the liquor influence was strong enough in the legislature to substitute license for prohibition. The consequence was an immediate increase of drunkenness and crime. Two years afterwards, the Secretary of State declared that "there was a greater increase of crime in one year under license than in seven years under prohibition."

Vineland, New Jersey, has a population of ten thousand. Absolute prohibition is the law of that community. One constable, who is also overseer of the poor, is sufficient to maintain public order. In 1875, his annual report says: "We have practically no debt. * * * The police expenses of Vineland amount to seventy-five dollars a year, the sum paid to me, and our poor expenses are a mere trifle."

In Potter County, Pennsylvania, there has been a prohibitory law for many years. Hon. John S. Mann says: "Its effect, as regards crime, is marked and conspicuous. *Our jail is without inmates, except the sheriff,* for more than half the time."

Other instances of local prohibition in this country could be given, but these are sufficient.

Bessbrook, a town in Ireland of four thousand inhabitants, has no liquor-shop, and whisky and strong drink are strictly prohibited. *There is no poor-house, pawn-shop or police-station.* The town is entirely free from strife, discord or disturbance.

In the county of Tyrone, Ireland, no drinking house is allowed. In 1870, Right Hon. Claude Hamilton said: "At present there is not a single policeman in that district. The poor-rates are half what they were before, and the magistrates testify to the great absence of crime."

In many parts of England and Scotland there is local prohibition, and the uniform testimony as to the absence of pauperism and crime is as unequivocal as that given above.

THE MAINE LAW—ITS COMPLETE VINDICATION.

But it is to the State of Maine, where a prohibitory law has existed for over a quarter of a century, and where prohibition has been put to the severest tests, that we must look for the more decisive proofs of success or failure.

On the evidence which Maine furnishes, the advocates of legal suppression are content to rest their case. In order to get a brief, but thoroughly accurate and reliable history of the Maine law, we addressed a letter to Hon. Neal Dow, of Portland, Maine, asking him to furnish us, for this volume, with the facts and evidence by which our readers could for themselves judge whether the law were a dead letter, as some asserted, or effective and salutory. In reply, Mr. Dow has kindly furnished us with the following deeply interesting and important communication:

TESTIMONY OF HON. NEAL DOW.

PORTLAND, October 12th, 1877.

T. S. ARTHUR, ESQ.:

Dear Sir—I will gladly furnish you with a brief history of the Maine Law, and a statement of its operation and effects in

Maine, in the hope that the wide circulation of the work you have in preparation may serve to correct the mistaken notion that prevails, to the effect that the law has failed of any useful result, and that the liquor traffic is carried on as extensively in Maine as ever it had been, with all its baleful effects upon the moral and material interests of the State.

In the old time the people of Maine were as much addicted to the use of strong drinks as those of any other part of the country; and the effects of this shocking habit were seen everywhere in shabby buildings, neglected farms and in wide-spread poverty. There were, in this State, magnificent forests of the best pine timber in the world. The manufacture of this timber into "lumber" of various descriptions, and the sale of it, were the leading industries of Maine. The products of our vast forests were sent chiefly to the West India Islands, and the returns were mostly in rum and in molasses, to be converted into rum by our own distilleries, of which there were many among us, in various parts of the State—seven of them in this city, running night and day. This rum, almost the whole of it, whether imported or home-made, was consumed among our own people. It was sent in the way of trade and in exchange for "lumber" into every part of our territory; not a town or village, or rural district escaped, however remote or thinly populated it might be.

The result of this was, that almost the entire value of all this vast industry went down the throats of our people in the shape of rum, either imported or home-made. I have heard men say who had been extensively engaged in this lumber trade, that Maine is not a dollar the richer, and never was, on account of this immense business; but that the people were poorer in consequence of it, and more miserable than they would have been if the pine forests had been swept away by a great conflagration.

The effects of this course of trade were seen everywhere throughout the State. In scarcely any part of it was there any evidence of business prosperity or thrift, but, generally, there was abundant evidence of poverty, untidiness and decay. In the lumbering towns and villages, where the innumerable saw-mills were, the greatest bustle and activity prevailed. The air resounded with the loud noises coming from these mills. Night and day they were "run," never ceasing until the "logs" were "worked up." Relays of hands were employed at all these lumbering centres, so that the saw-mills never stopped even for an hour during "the season," except for some occasional repairs. All these men drank rum; a quart a day per man was a moderate quantity; but a great many of them required two quarts a day. The result of this was, that the entire wages of the men were consumed in drink, except a meagre share that went to the miserable wives and children at home.

Everywhere throughout the State the results of this way of life was to be seen—in the general poverty of the people, and in the shabbiness of all their surroundings. But some persons conceived the idea that all this evil was not necessary and inevitable; that it came from the liquor traffic, which might be prohibited and suppressed, as lottery-tickets, gambling-houses and impure books and pictures had already been. And they devoted themselves constantly and industriously to the work of correcting the public opinion of the people as to the liquor traffic by demonstrating to them that this trade was in deadly hostility to every interest of the State, while no good came from it, nor could come from it, to State or people.

This educational work was carried on persistently for years; meetings were held by these persons in every little country-church and town-house, and in every little wayside school-house, where the farmers and their wives and children assembled at the call of these missionaries, to listen to their burning denunciation of the liquor traffic, which lived only by spreading poverty, pauperism, suffering, insanity, crime and premature death broadcast over the State. The result of this teaching was, that the public opinion of the State became thoroughly changed as to the character of the liquor traffic and its relation to the public prosperity and welfare.

When we thought the time had come for it, we demanded of the Legislature that the law of "license," then upon the statute books, which represented the public opinion of the old time, should be changed for a law of prohibition, representing the improved public opinion of the present time; and, after two unsuccessful attempts to procure such a law, we obtained what we desired, an act of absolute prohibition to the manufacture and sale of strong drink—a measure for which we had labored long and industriously for many years.

At the time of the enactment of this statute, now known as the MAINE LAW the world over, the liquor traffic was carried on extensively in the State, wholesale and retail, precisely as it is now in New York, New Jersey, Pennsylvania and in every other State where that trade is licensed and protected by the law. The Maine Law went into operation immediately upon its approval by the Governor, and by its provisions, liquors kept for sale everywhere, all over the State, were liable to be seized, forfeited and destroyed, and the owners to be punished by fine and imprisonment. The municipal authorities of the cities and towns allowed the dealers a reasonable time to send away their stocks of liquors to other States and countries, where their sale was permitted by the law.

The liquor-traders availed themselves of this forbearance of the authorities, and did generally send their stock of liquors out of the State. The open sale of liquors came instantly to an end throughout all our territory, and where it continued, it was done secretly, as other things are done in violation of law. The manufacture of intoxicating liquors was entirely stopped, so that in all the State there was absolutely none produced, except cider, which might be made and used for vinegar.

The effect of this policy of prohibition to the liquor traffic was speedily visible in our work-houses, jails and houses of corrections. The jail of Cumberland County, the most populous of the State, had been badly over-crowded, but within four months of the enactment of the law there were but five prisoners in it, three of whom were liquor-sellers, put in for violation of the law. The jails of Penobscot; Kennebec, Franklin, Oxford and York were absolutely empty. The inmates of the work-houses were greatly reduced in number, and in some of the smaller towns pauperism ceased entirely.

But, during all this time, in every part of the country, reports were industriously circulated that the law was inoperative for good, and that liquors were sold in Maine as freely and in as large quantities as before the law. These false statements were industriously and persistently made everywhere by those interested in the liquor trade, and by those impelled by appetite or passion. It is sufficient for me to say here that the Maine Law, from the first, has been as faithfully executed as our other criminal laws have been, though there has been, at certain times, and in certain localities, considerable complicity with the violators of it, on the part of many officers of the law, so that the Legislature has at last provided heavy penalties for the punishment of prosecuting officers, justices of the peace and judges of municipal and police courts, in case of failure in their duty. I am glad to be able to say that the judges of our higher courts have, from the first, been true to their duty in the administration of this law, as of all others.

In much the larger part of Maine, in all the rural districts, in the villages and smaller towns, the liquor traffic is absolutely unknown; no such thing as a liquor-shop exists there, either open or secret. The traffic lingers secretly only in the larger towns and cities, where it leads a precarious and troubled life—only among the lowest and vilest part of our foreign population. Nowhere in the State is there any visible sign of this horrible trade. The penalties of the law, as they now stand, are sufficient to extinguish the traffic in all the small towns, and to drive it into dens and dark corners in the larger towns. The people of Maine now regard this trade as living, where it exists at all, only on the misery and wretchedness of the community. They speak of it everywhere, in the press, on the platform, and in legislative halls, as the gigantic crime of crimes, and we mean to treat it as such by the law.

For some years after the enactment of the law, it entered largely into the politics of the State. Candidates were nominated by one party or the other with reference to their proclivities for rum or their hostility to it, and the people were determined in their votes, one way or the other, by this consideration.

Now, the policy of prohibition, with penalties stringent enough to be effective, has become as firmly settled in this State as that of universal education or the vote by ballot. The Republican party, in its annual conventions, during all these years, has affirmed, unanimously, its "adhesion to prohibition and the vigorous enforcement of laws to that end;" and the Democratic party, in its annual convention of this year, rejected, by an immense majority, and with enthusiastic cheers, a resolution, proposed from the floor, in favor of "license."

The original Maine Law was enacted by a vote in the House of eighty-six to forty, and in the Senate by eighteen to ten. There have been several subsequent liquor laws, all in the direction of greater stringency; and the Legislature of this year enacted an additional law, with penalties much more stringent than any which had preceded it, without a dissenting vote. No one can mistake the significance of this fact; it was an unanimous affirmation of adhesion to the policy of prohibition, after a steady trial of it and experience of its results for more than a quarter of a century. And, since that time, the people have passed upon it at the late annual election by an approval of the policy and of the men who favor it—by an immense majority. If it be conceded that the people of Maine possess an ordinary share of intelligence and common sense, this result would be impossible, unless the effect of prohibition had been beneficial to the State and to them.

While we were earnestly at work in bringing up the public opinion of the State to the point of demanding the prohibition of the liquor traffic, as a more important political and social question than any other or all others, I was startled at hearing a gentleman of the town of Raymond declare that in his town the people consumed in strong drink its entire valuation in every period of eighteen years eight months and twenty-five days! "Here are the figures," he said; "I know the quantity of liquor brought into the town annually. I am so situated that I am able to state this accurately, beyond all possibility of doubt, except that liquors may be brought here by other than the ordinary mode of transportation without my knowledge; but the quantities stated in this paper (which he held in his hand), and their cost are within my knowledge." This was part of a speech to his fellow-townsmen, and his statement was admitted to be true. Now there is not a drop of liquor sold in that town, and there has not been any sold there for many years. This statement may strike us at first blush to be tremendously exaggerated, that the people of any locality should consume in strong drink the entire value of its real estate and personal property in every period of less than twenty years. But let us examine it.

We learn from the Bureau of Statistics that the annual liquor bill of the United States is seven hundred millions of dollars. This does not include the enormous quantity of "crooked whisky" which has been put upon the market with or without the knowledge, consent, assent or complicity of our public officers, from the highest to the lowest. The drink bill of the United Kingdom, with a population smaller than ours, is more than this by many millions. This valuation—seven hundred millions of dollars—is the price, by the quantity, taken from the figures as they come into the public office, while the cost to the consumers is vastly greater. Now, this sum with annual compound interest for ten years, amounts to the enormous figure of eight billions nine hundred and forty-four millions one hundred and forty-one thousands of dollars—almost nine thousand millions of dollars! For twenty years the amount is twenty-five billions two hundred and forty-five millions six hundred and eighty-one thousands of dollars. Twenty-five thousand two hundred and forty-five millions of dollars and more; actually as much, within a fraction, as the entire value of the personal and landed property of the United States! My friend of Raymond may well be credited in the statement made to his fellow-townsmen.

Now, as the result of the Maine Law, in Maine, the wealth and prosperity of the people have greatly increased. This can be seen in every part of the State, and is obvious to the most casual observer who knew what Maine was before the law of prohibition and knows what it has been since and down to the present time. Evidences of industry, enterprise and thrift everywhere, instead of the general poverty, unthrift and shabbiness of the old rum-time.

The share of Maine of the National drink-bill would be about thirteen millions of dollars, and but for the Maine Law, we should be consuming our full proportion; but now I feel myself fully warranted in saying that we do not expend in that way one-tenth of that sum. A mayor of the city of Portland, in a message to the City Council, said: "The quantity of liquor now sold is not one-fiftieth part as much as it was before the enactment of the law." The difference, whatever it may be, between the sum we should waste in strong drink, but for the law, and that which we actually squander in that way, we have in our pockets, in our savings banks and in our business, so that Maine has suffered far less, financially, during this crisis than any other part of the country.

I have said the drink-bill of Maine, but for prohibition, would be about thirteen millions of dollars annually, in proportion to that of the whole country. Now, this sum, with annual compound interest at six per cent., in ten years will amount to one hundred and seventy millions three hundred and nineteen thousand five hundred and twenty-eight dollars, and in twenty years to four hundred and sixty-three millions eight hundred and fifty-four thousand four hundred and twenty dollars—more than twice the entire valuation of the State by the estimate made in 1870, which was two hundred and twenty-four millions eight hundred and twenty-two thousand nine hundred and thirteen dollars. There was a reason then for the fact, that in the old rum-time the people of Maine were poor and unthrifty in every way—and for that other fact, that now they are prosperous and flourishing, with a better business than that of any other State, proportionately.

Notwithstanding the fact that in Portland a great conflagration destroyed ten millions of dollars in 1866, burned down half the town, and turned ten thousand people out of doors, the prosperity of the city has been steadily on the increase. Its valuation, in 1860, was twenty-one millions eight hundred and sixty-six thousand dollars, and in 1870, twenty-nine millions four hundred and thirty-nine thousand two hundred and fifty-seven dollars. In the last year the increase in valuation, in spite of the hard times, was four hundred and eighty thousand dollars, while Boston, with free rum, has lost more than eight millions, and New York and Brooklyn has experienced an immense depreciation.

I think I have said enough to satisfy every intelligent, unprejudiced man that the absolute prohibition and suppression of the liquor traffic has been in the highest interest of our State and people. I am very truly, yours,

NEAL DOW.

And here we close our discussion of the most important of all the social questions that are to-day before the people; and, in doing so, declare it as our solemn conviction, that until the liquor traffic is abolished, and the evils with which it curses the people removed, all efforts at moral reforms must languish, and the Church find impediments in her way which cannot be removed. The CURSE is upon us, and there is but one CURE: *Total Abstinence*, by the help of God, for the individual, and *Prohibition* for the State.

www.ingramcontent.com/pod-product-compliance
Lightning Source LLC
LaVergne TN
LVHW020228110826
845151LV00003B/859

* 9 7 8 1 4 2 5 5 3 1 1 4 0 *